CURRY&
KIMCHI

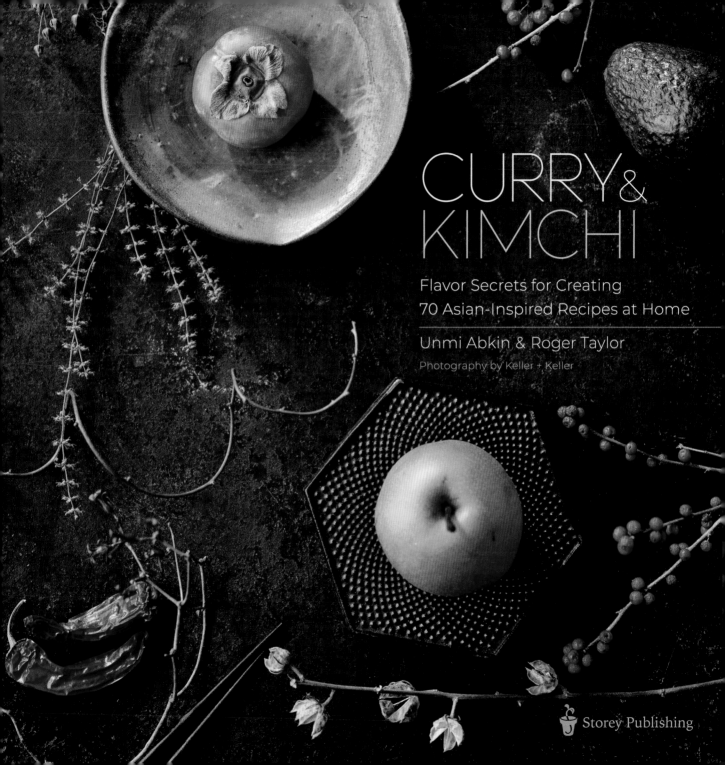

CURRY & KIMCHI

Flavor Secrets for Creating
70 Asian-Inspired Recipes at Home

Unmi Abkin & Roger Taylor

Photography by Keller + Keller

Storey Publishing

The mission of Storey Publishing is to serve our customers by publishing practical information that encourages personal independence in harmony with the environment.

EDITED BY Deanna F. Cook and Sarah Guare

ART DIRECTION AND BOOK DESIGN BY Carolyn Eckert

TEXT PRODUCTION BY Liseann Karandisecky and Erin Dawson

INDEXED BY Christine R. Lindemer, Boston Road Communications

COVER PHOTOGRAPHY BY © Keller + Keller Photography, except authors' photograph, inside back by © Cara Totman

INTERIOR PHOTOGRAPHY BY © Keller + Keller Photography

ADDITIONAL PHOTOGRAPHY BY © Cara Totman, 9, 10 bottom, 11 top, 16, 17 top left, 42 top left, 170 and © Roger Taylor, 11 bottom, 17 bottom left, 156 top right, 160, 161 bottom left

FOOD STYLING BY Unmi Abkin and Roger Taylor

PROP AND PHOTO STYLING BY Ann Lewis

ADDITIONAL PROP AND RESTAURANT STYLING BY Donn Boulanger

TEXT © 2019 BY Unmi Abkin and Roger Taylor

Storey books are available at special discounts when purchased in bulk for premiums and sales promotions as well as for fund-raising or educational use. Special editions or book excerpts can also be created to specification. For details, please call 800-827-8673, or send an email to sales@storey.com.

Storey Publishing
210 MASS MoCA Way
North Adams, MA 01247
storey.com

Printed in China through Asia Pacific Offset

10 9 8 7 6 5 4 3 2 1

Library of Congress Cataloging-in-Publication Data on file

DEDICATED
to Guy and Jeanine
Saperstein, who have
helped so many, including us,
to follow their dreams.

CONTENTS

PART 1:
DRESSINGS AND SALADS
21

PART 2:
SAUCES AND SALSAS WITH MAIN DISHES
47

PART 3:
CONDIMENTS, PICKLES, AND INFUSED OILS
127

Korean Hot Pepper Dressing 23
Grilled Shrimp, Asian Pear,
and Watercress Salad 24

Honey Miso Dressing 26
Honey Miso Noodle Salad 28

Jalapeño Lime Dressing 31
Orange, Mango,
and Avocado Salad 32

Orange Ginger Vinaigrette 35
Chinese Chicken Salad 36

Togarashi Dressing 39
Broccoli Salad 40

Red Wine Vinaigrette 43
Zesty Jalapeño Cabbage Slaw 44

Spicy Szechuan Peanut Sauce 49
Dan Dan Noodles 50

INSTANT POT RECIPES:

Manchamanteles Salsa 53
Pork Carnitas Tacos 54

Scallion Ginger Jam 56
Clay Pot Miso Chicken 58

Shoyu Ramen Broth and Tare 60
Coco Shoyu Ramen 65

Hoisin Barbecue Sauce 66
Hoisin-Glazed Baby Back Ribs 68

Plum Sauce 71
East-West Rice Bowl 72

Korean Hot Pepper Sauce 74
Grilled Short Rib Tacos 76
Bibimbap 78

Thai Peanut Sauce 81
Thai Chicken Rice Bowl 82

Korean Bolognese 85
Korean Spaghetti 86
Korean Sloppy Joes 88

Chow Fun Sauce 91
Coriander Shrimp Chow Fun 92

General Tso's Sauce 95
General Tso's Tofu 96

Vegan Coconut Curry 99
Steamed Kabocha Squash and
Tofu Rice Bowl 100

Cilantro Salsa Verde 103
Chili Con Carne 104

Green Thai Curry 107
Salmon and Green Thai Curry
Rice Bowl 108

Ponzu 111
Miso-Glazed Cod Rice Bowl 112

Teriyaki Sauce 115
Salmon Teriyaki Bento Box 116

Phad Thai Sauce 118
Shiitake Mushroom and
Tofu Phad Thai 119

Mornay 122
Macaroni and Cheese 124

Spicy Miso Paste 128
Lime Shallot Crème Fraîche 130
Thai Cabbage 133
Kalbi Marinade 134
Soy-Cured Eggs 136
Miso Marinade 139
Seasoned Bean Sprouts 140
Seasoned Carrots 140
Pickled White Onions 142
Quick Kimchi 145

Xander's Cucumber Pickles 146
Pickled Shiitake Mushrooms 149
Pickled Japanese Turnips 150
Pickled Ginger 152
Ginger Oil 152
Chive Oil 154
Chile Oil 154
Togarashi Oil 156
Seasoned Rice Wine Vinegar 157
Szechuan Oil 158

EVERYDAY EQUIPMENT 160

EVERYDAY INGREDIENTS 162

THANK YOU 170

INDEX 171

METRIC CONVERSION CHARTS 176

KEY:

Dressings, Sauces, and Salsas / IN BLACK
Salads and Main Dishes / IN RED

OUR
ROOTS

UNMI

I REALLY WISH I could tell you something about my mother, but she left soon after I was born. I'd like to think she was a good cook. My story started in South Korea, as part of a family that struggled to keep a roof overhead and dinner on the table. My father was a neon sign artist and an alcoholic. My older sister, Sunmi, cared for me as well as she could during the long stretches when my father was unable to do so.

A huge part of my relationship to food has to do with the lack of it. My family wasn't wealthy or even particularly stable. More often than not, we were homeless and hungry. In the last few months before I was sent to an orphanage, we sometimes slept on rooftops and searched for food wherever we could find it.

One of my first memories of food is when I was four or five, staring at a fruit stand across the street from where I was waiting for my sister. Bananas were piled up on a table, and I had never seen anything like them before. I knew they were food because they were stacked near fruits that I recognized; I just had no idea what they were. I was pretty sure they would be amazing and I really wanted one. I think of this often when I eat a banana. I don't take it for granted.

When I was six or seven, I was adopted by a Jewish American man and a Mexican woman and eventually moved to the United States. I soaked in the Jewish food traditions of my father's

family and spent summers with my mother's family in Mexico. To this day, I have a soft spot for hamantaschen and pan dulces, as they represent the acceptance and love of my new family, in two new countries.

My families, then and now, gave me the strength and will to follow my passion, food, wherever it led me — from California to France, Morocco, and Massachusetts. They supported me when I spent countless hours in professional kitchens across the country, learning and absorbing whatever I could in order to make and capture new memories of food, and when I opened three restaurants of my own.

I never thought much about writing a cookbook until I reflected on my distinctive food heritage and I realized that I did indeed have my own special and unique perspective on food. My experiences both as a chef and as a mother have shaped the way I cook, creating food that is clear and vibrant, simple and easy to execute, and — above all — delicious.

ROGER

MY FATHER IS A BAKER and my cousin is a chef, so some of my earliest memories are the sights and sounds of professional kitchens: crashing pans and silverware on plates, and more often than not, cursing (sometimes in several languages). I started working in restaurants when I was 15, washing dishes, and I never looked back.

One doesn't survive in the restaurant industry for long without developing an eye for efficiency. There is a subtle art to creating a menu that dazzles while still being sustainable for the people producing it. This skill has served me well in my 17-year working relationship with Unmi, and in our 14-year marriage. Between Unmi's passion for flavor and feeding people and my ability to pare unnecessary steps and ingredients without sacrificing the soul of a dish, we have created a book full of recipes that we are proud of. We hope they become a part of your life the way they have become a part of ours.

COCO

I'M LUCKY to be growing up in a restaurant like my dad did, and I feel proud that it is named after me! Some of these recipes have been my favorites for years, like the mac and cheese. I like it so much that one time when I was in preschool, I invited my whole class for lunch without telling my parents. Uh-oh! I taste-tested almost all of the things in this book, and they are really good for kids!

THE SECRET INGREDIENT

Seasoned Rice Wine Vinegar

You'll see that a number of recipes in this book contain seasoned rice wine vinegar. The key to many Asian dishes is finding a balance between salt, sweet, and acid, and nothing delivers all three quite like seasoned rice wine vinegar.

Why are these elements of flavor so important? Acid and salt amplify other flavors, and the sweetness helps balance out salt and acid. You can certainly purchase a bottle at the store, but we rely on this unique and potent blend so much that we have been making our own using organic rice wine vinegar and honey instead of sugar (see recipe on page 157). Don't underestimate the power of adding a splash to a sauce or dressing that needs a little something extra to make it sing!

COCO PRINCIPLES

This book represents a chance for us to relate some of our accumulated knowledge and experience from decades of working together in our restaurants, including our present restaurant, Coco and the Cellar Bar, in Easthampton, Massachusetts. Our success lies in our ability to simply execute clarity of flavor. Our straightforward methodology is easy for the home cook as well, and we hope to inspire you to create exciting, flavorful, globally inspired food in your own kitchens. We have enjoyed creating this book immensely and are delighted to share some of our philosophies for creating memorable meals for family and friends. In the back of this book (see pages 160–169) you will find lists of our everyday equipment and ingredients that help us make these dishes at home.

SEASONING
One of the most important things an inexperienced cook at Coco must learn is to have a healthy respect for the power of proper seasoning. We tell these young cooks that the key to maximizing flavor and texture is to understand exactly what a given amount of salt will do. That understanding comes over time, usually with sometimes comic, sometimes tragic, results.

A Note on Alternative Sweeteners

One of the most profound shifts in cooking today is the use of sweetener alternatives in place of refined sugar. Cooks are making the switch for a number of reasons, including health and sustainability. We prefer mild honey, like clover or wildflower honey, and coconut nectar because they don't have a large impact on the flavor profile of a dish. Wherever it makes sense, we have included sugar alternatives.

One way to increase the odds of success is to use the same type of salt every time you cook, so that you can become familiar with it. We prefer Diamond Crystal Kosher Salt for seasoning during the cooking process, and Maldon Sea Salt Flakes for finishing plates. We find Diamond Crystal to be a pure, consistent product, and because of the flake shape of the grains, a packed teaspoon of Diamond Crystal contains considerably less salt than a packed teaspoon of table or sea salt. This means there is less chance of over-salting your dishes as you are getting used to your salt. Maldon is a much more delicate and flakier salt. Just a few flakes sprinkled over the top of a dish adds an unmistakable crunch and pop of salinity that really wakes up a plate.

BALANCE

A principal concept that sets the food at Coco apart is the constant pursuit of balance. We look at the interaction between six components — salt, spice, fat, acid, sweet, and umami — and try to find balance among them. It is easy for most people to identify when a bite is too salty or too acidic; too spicy or cloyingly sweet. When these aspects of flavor are working together, however, most people don't notice the balance — they just recognize it as delicious. The cooks at Coco all have to ask themselves over and over, "What is this missing?" or "Why does this still taste flat?" Making delicious food requires a great deal of tasting, and just as much critical examination. A perfect example of these principles at play is a well-made bowl of ramen (see pages 18 and 19).

A Note on Umami

Umami is a combination of the Japanese words for "delicious" and "taste" and describes a very primal savoriness that we associate with Parmesan cheese, mushrooms, steak, tomatoes, anchovies, olives, and — especially — ketchup. The most famous (or infamous) chemically manufactured source of umami is MSG or monosodium glutamate, but there are plenty of other man-made sources of glutamate as well, like soy sauce and fish sauce.

PLANNING Making good food isn't usually the result of some epiphany, where the first time you try something it works perfectly and the recipe is set in stone. We all have to assess how well something works the first time we try it and adjust accordingly the next time. By planning ahead and prepping some ingredients the day before, we can make sure everything comes together on the plate in a timely fashion.

PRESENTATION Presenting food in an appealing and attractive fashion can be as tricky as preparing it properly. Arranging a plate requires a light touch and a confidence that comes from lots of experience. In order to take some of the guesswork out of presentation, we have included four-step progression photos for many of the recipes. These will give some insight into how we approach plate construction — and some inspiration for your own plates!

JOY We'll be the first to admit that it isn't easy to keep the stresses of the modern world from affecting our outlook on life, but our frame of mind has a profound effect on our cooking. If you are angry or preoccupied, you are more likely to skip steps or miss the subtle cues that can be the difference between a good meal and a great one. We try to maintain a sense of gratitude and joy about our circumstances, and we try to remember how lucky we are to be able to do what we love and feed our friends, family, and guests.

FLAVOR BALANCE AND SAUCES

A bowl of ramen is a perfect example of the importance of flavor balance. The deep meatiness of the chicken and pork broth needs the contrast of the salty sea elements in the dashi, and both of those need to be balanced by the umami-packed tare (see page 60). The toppings add important layers as well — from the sweet brightness of the pickled shiitake mushrooms to the creamy fattiness of the soy-cured egg and the spice from the togarashi oil. We've spent years perfecting the flavor components of the dishes in this book, so that they will come together perfectly each time.

Our ramen recipe is also a great example of how a well-crafted sauce embraces and supports the main ingredients in a dish. We think the foundation that is laid by a well-balanced sauce is so important that we have organized the recipes in this book around the sauces. We first provide a recipe for a sauce, and then present a dish that includes that sauce.

BROTH

DASHI

TARE

FAT

ACID

SALT

SPICE

SWEET

UMAMI

PART 1

DRESSINGS AND SALADS

These salads are just as good as those in our restaurant, but they are particularly favorable to the home cook thanks to sturdier ingredients like broccoli or noodles and dressings that you can make a day or two ahead of time.

KOREAN HOT PEPPER DRESSING

The flavors in this dressing — slightly sweet, somewhat spicy, and rounded out by the sesame oil — remind us of the little house salads you get at Korean or Japanese restaurants. It is strong enough to stand up to the grilled shrimp in our **Grilled Shrimp, Asian Pear, and Watercress Salad** (page 24).

1. STIR together in a large bowl, then let macerate for 30 minutes:
   - ½ cup Seasoned Rice Wine Vinegar (page 157)
   - ¼ cup lime juice
   - 1½ tablespoons lemon juice
   - 1 tablespoon minced shallots
   - 1 clove garlic, minced
   - 2 teaspoons gochugaru (page 164)
   - 2 teaspoons mild honey
   - ½ teaspoon toasted sesame seeds

2. WHISK in slowly:
   - ¼ cup neutral cooking oil
   - ½ teaspoon toasted sesame oil
   - ½ teaspoon Togarashi Oil (page 156)

TOPPING FOR RICE

At the restaurant, we noticed a cook drizzle some of this dressing over a bowl of rice topped with toasted nuts and sliced avocados. We thought it made a fantastic pre-dinner snack!

YIELD: 1 CUP

STORAGE: This dressing will keep in the refrigerator for up to 7 days.

GRILLED SHRIMP, ASIAN PEAR, AND WATERCRESS SALAD

Impromptu salads are the best salads. In season, just about any salad can be modified depending on what is available. This salad is a perfect example of that. If you can't find Asian pears, use Bosc pears — or any ripe, sweet, and juicy pears for that matter. Persimmons would be beautiful too. We've even replaced the shrimp with roasted shiitake mushrooms to great success.

1. PREHEAT grill to high heat.

2. COMBINE in a large bowl:
   - 1 pound shrimp, peeled and cleaned
   - 2 tablespoons neutral cooking oil
   - Salt

3. SEASON shrimp well with salt and toss to coat. Carefully place shrimp on grill grates and cook for 2 minutes. Flip and cook for 1 to 2 minutes longer. Remove shrimp to a plate and allow to cool.

4. FAN out on the serving plate:
   - ¼ Asian pear, thinly sliced

5. COVER with:
   - 1 cup watercress

6. TOP the watercress with the grilled shrimp.

7. DRIZZLE over the salad:
   - 2 tablespoons Korean Hot Pepper Dressing (page 23)

8. FINISH the salad with:
   - 1 scallion, sliced
   - ½ teaspoon toasted sesame seeds
   - Pinch of flaky sea salt

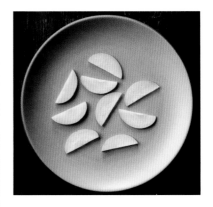

PLATING
PROGRESSION PHOTOS
One of the most fun and important parts of cooking is presentation. You might have heard that people eat with their eyes as well as their mouths. When a dish looks beautiful, we begin to salivate for it — preparing ourselves to eat it. How a food looks can be just as important as how it tastes. Where it makes sense, we have included progression plating photos to help you present the dish beautifully.

YIELD: 4 SERVINGS

HONEY MISO DRESSING

This dressing is remarkably stable and can certainly last a week in the refrigerator. We recommend making the dressing a day or two ahead, so the flavors have ample time to come together. Store it in a large squeeze bottle so that you can easily add it to the **Honey Miso Noodle Salad** (page 28) when you are ready. You can also drizzle it over grilled asparagus or salmon and top with some sesame seeds!

1. WHISK together in a large bowl:
   - ½ cup white miso
   - ½ cup Seasoned Rice Wine Vinegar (page 157)
   - ¼ cup honey
   - 2 tablespoons tamari
   - 1 clove garlic, minced
   - 1 teaspoon minced ginger
   - ½ teaspoon toasted sesame oil

2. WHISK in slowly:
   - 1 cup neutral cooking oil

DRESSING AS DIP

If you are as tired as we are of onion dip and ranch dressing with crudité, we recommend using this dressing as a dip. It is a breath of fresh air at parties, and people always notice it.

YIELD: 2 CUPS

STORAGE: This dressing will keep in the refrigerator for up to 7 days.

HONEY MISO NOODLE SALAD

It is hard to overestimate how large a role this noodle salad has played in our lives. It has been a bestseller at two of our restaurants, and everybody complains when we take it off the menu in wintertime. It's quick and casual enough for lunch and substantial enough for dinner. Its beauty lies in its subtlety — it isn't an in-your-face dish — and kids love it (especially without the cilantro).

1. **COMBINE** in a large mixing bowl and toss until evenly dressed:

   6   ounces lo mein egg noodles, cooked al dente
   2   cups shaved green cabbage
   2   cups chopped cooked chicken
   2   medium carrots, peeled and julienned (1 cup)
   1   cup arugula
   ¼   cup chopped cilantro
   ½   cup Honey Miso Dressing (page 26)

2. **PORTION** salad into four serving bowls. To finish, divide among the four bowls:

   ¼   cup thinly sliced scallions
   1   tablespoon toasted sesame seeds
        Pinch of red pepper flakes

MAKE IT GLUTEN-FREE
For a gluten-free version, omit the egg noodles or replace them with a brown rice pasta. You could also serve it with cubes of extra-firm tofu in place of chicken.

YIELD: 4 SERVINGS

JALAPEÑO LIME DRESSING

We love salad dressings that check off a lot of flavor boxes. This one fits the bill for sure. It has the spicy-sweet-tart balance we are always looking for, and because it has been emulsified, it has a creamy texture that rounds out the sharp acidic edges. It works beautifully on the **Orange, Mango, and Avocado Salad** (page 32).

1. COMBINE in a blender:
     1   teaspoon minced shallots
     ¼   jalapeño, seeded and diced
     1   clove garlic, sliced
          Zest of ½ lime
     3   tablespoons lime juice
     3   tablespoons Seasoned Rice Wine Vinegar (page 157)
     1   tablespoon mild honey
     ½   teaspoon ground coriander
     ¼   teaspoon kosher salt
     ½   cup neutral cooking oil

2. BLEND ingredients on high until well combined.

TRY IT ON CORN

At the height of summer, we grill fresh-picked corn and brush this dressing on after it comes off the grill; it's a great alternative to butter!

YIELD: ¾ CUP

STORAGE: This dressing will keep in the refrigerator for up to 7 days.

ORANGE, MANGO, AND AVOCADO SALAD

The citrus and avocado salad, with nearly limitless room for seasonal variation, is a classic Northern California dish. This salad isn't tossed or arranged in layers. The key is to make it pretty without seeming to try too hard.

1. SLICE the tops and bottoms off:
   2 oranges

2. REMOVE the rind and pith of the oranges with the knife in clean arcs, then slice into ¼-inch rounds. Divide the orange slices between four plates, arranging in an even layer.

3. PLACE on a cutting board, holding it lengthwise:
   1 mango

4. SLICE the mango into three pieces lengthwise, so that you have two meaty side pieces and a center slice containing the pit. Using a large spoon, scoop the flesh from the side pieces and cut into 1½-inch cubes. Using a paring knife, cut the skin away from the middle slice, cut around the pit, then cut the remaining flesh into 1½-inch cubes.

5. PLACE the mango pieces in a medium bowl and toss with:
   1 tablespoon lime juice

6. SCATTER the mango pieces on top of the orange slices. Cut in half lengthwise, around the pit:
   1 avocado

7. SCOOP out the pit, then remove the avocado flesh from the skin with a large spoon. Slice into half moons, and distribute evenly among the four plates.

8. TOP each plate with:
   ½ cup baby arugula

9. DRIZZLE each plate with:
   2–3 tablespoons Jalapeño Lime Dressing (page 31)

10. FINISH with flaky sea salt.

MIX IT UP

No good citrus available?
Use roasted and pickled beets,
or even sweet, ripe tomatoes!
Avocados no good? Don't use them!
A shaved cheese like ricotta
salata (see page 168) can provide
that creaminess. Add some nice
crab meat to make it a light meal.

YIELD: 4 SERVINGS

ORANGE GINGER VINAIGRETTE

This vinaigrette has all the brashness and strength of a typical dressing for **Chinese Chicken Salad** (page 36) but without the cloying, sugary sweetness and oppressive soy notes. After a lot of trial and error, we settled on orange juice concentrate. It's a great way to add a velvety texture and body, and it also replaces the ubiquitous syrupy canned mandarin oranges you normally find in Chinese chicken salad.

1. COMBINE in a blender:
   - ¼ cup frozen orange juice (defrosted)
   - 2 tablespoons lime juice
   - 2 tablespoons soy sauce
   - 3 tablespoons Seasoned Rice Wine Vinegar (page 157)
   - 1 tablespoon chopped ginger
   - ¼ cup neutral cooking oil
   - 1 tablespoon chopped scallion
   - 2 tablespoons chopped cilantro
   - 1 teaspoon toasted sesame oil

2. BLEND all ingredients until well combined.

YIELD: 1 CUP

STORAGE: This dressing will keep in the refrigerator for up to 3 days.

CHINESE CHICKEN SALAD

This recipe is our attempt to take back the Chinese chicken salad, which is commonly found in airport takeaway cases or convention center catering menus. It typically comes with peanuts, but we use Marcona almonds and Szechuan oil to give it a more sophisticated look and feel.

1. **COMBINE** in a large bowl:

2	chicken breasts, cooked and shredded (about 3 cups)
1	large carrot, peeled and cut into matchsticks
4	scallions, sliced on a bias
½	head napa cabbage, shaved
¼	cup Xander's Cucumber Pickles (page 146), cut into half moons
¼	cup chopped cilantro
2	tablespoons chopped Marcona almonds
1	tablespoon toasted sesame seeds

2. **ADD** to salad:

   3–4 tablespoons Orange Ginger Vinaigrette (page 35)

3. **TOSS** salad well. Add more dressing as desired and adjust seasoning to taste with:

   Flaky sea salt
   Szechuan Oil (page 158)

QUICK CHICKEN

Traditionally, Chinese chicken salad is made from chicken that has been poached, then cooled and shredded, but who has time for that? This is a fantastic way to use a rotisserie chicken from your local supermarket. Just let it cool before you shred it, and you have just saved yourself 30 minutes of cooking and cleaning!

YIELD: 4 SERVINGS

TOGARASHI DRESSING

Most of the time, you make a salad dressing to highlight a particular vinegar or an ingredient in the salad. We love our togarashi oil so much that this was the first time we made a dressing to showcase the oil. We created our **Broccoli Salad** (page 40) specifically for this dressing.

COMBINE in a small bowl:

¼ cup Seasoned Rice Wine Vinegar (page 157)
1 tablespoon soy sauce
1 tablespoon toasted sesame oil
1 scallion, thinly sliced
1 tablespoon Pickled Ginger (page 152), finely chopped
¼ cup Togarashi Oil (page 156)

SUSHI LOVE

Our daughter Coco loves to spoon some of this dressing over sushi rolls. This is the first, but certainly not the last, innovation in this book that came from a grade-schooler.

YIELD: ¾ CUP

STORAGE: This dressing will keep in the refrigerator for up to 7 days.

BROCCOLI SALAD

We took the template of the basic American broccoli salad and replaced elements until we had something with a much more Japanese angle. The toasted pine nuts take the place of walnuts, and the chopped pickled ginger in the dressing replaces the sweet and tart flavor of dried cranberries. We omit the mayonnaise for a bright, fresh new salad. Serve this as a side dish with our **General Tso's Tofu** (page 96).

1. CUT into small florets:
   - 1 head broccoli (3 cups florets)

2. DISCARD the broccoli stems and prepare an ice bath.

3. BRING a medium pot of salted water to a boil. Blanch the broccoli until bright green and just cooked through, about 1 minute. Use a slotted spoon to transfer the broccoli to the ice bath to stop cooking. Once cool, remove from the ice bath and drain well.

4. PLACE the broccoli in a large bowl, and add:
   - ¼ cup toasted pine nuts
   - 3 tablespoons Togarashi Dressing (page 39)

5. TOSS well to combine.

DRYING TIP
Use a salad spinner to drain the broccoli after blanching and cooling. Our friend and colleague Aaron Thayer hit upon this as we were developing this recipe, and it makes a world of difference in the finished salad.

YIELD: 4 SERVINGS

RED WINE VINAIGRETTE

This very basic French vinaigrette is made from ingredients you likely already have on hand. It is a great first recipe for little cooks. It is perfect in our **Zesty Jalapeño Cabbage Slaw** (page 44) or as a dressing for a simple garden lettuce salad or a summer salad of tomatoes, cucumber, fresh basil, and olive oil croutons.

1. COMBINE in a small bowl or a jar with a lid:
   - 1 teaspoon Dijon mustard
   - 1 small clove garlic, cracked once with the side of a knife
   - ¼ cup red wine vinegar
   - ⅛ teaspoon kosher salt

2. LET ingredients steep for 20 minutes Remove and discard the cracked garlic clove. Stir into the bowl:
   - ½ cup plus 2 tablespoons neutral oil
   - 1 tablespoon extra-virgin olive oil

3. WHISK or shake vigorously to combine.

YIELD: ¾ CUP

STORAGE: This vinaigrette will keep in the refrigerator for at least 7 days.

ZESTY JALAPEÑO CABBAGE SLAW

We serve this slaw at our restaurant with all sorts of things —
most notably our mac and cheese and our fried chicken.
It has to be brash and bright in order to serve as a counterpoint
to the creaminess of those dishes.

1. TOSS well to combine in a large bowl, then set aside for
   20 minutes:
   - ½ head green cabbage, finely shredded
   - ½ teaspoon salt

2. COMBINE and macerate in a small bowl for 20 minutes:
   - ¼ small red onion, thinly sliced
   - 2 tablespoons red wine vinegar

3. ADD to the cabbage and toss very well to combine:
   - Macerated onions, drained
   - 2 tablespoons chopped cilantro
   - ½ jalapeño pepper, seeded and sliced thin
   - 2 tablespoons Red Wine Vinaigrette (page 43)

DOUBLE IT

*We suggest doubling the recipe
because you are going to
want seconds of this slaw for
tacos, side dishes, and the like.
Leftovers will keep in the
refrigerator for up to 2 days.*

YIELD: 4 SERVINGS

SAUCES AND SALSAS WITH MAIN DISHES

We firmly believe that the backbone of many great dinners is a great sauce. We suggest making the sauces a day ahead so your dinner prep will be much more manageable.

SPICY SZECHUAN PEANUT SAUCE

We first caught the Szechuan bug after a wonderful meal at Mission Chinese in San Francisco. Knowing that the unique, tingling spiciness could be a little intimidating, we set out to find a gentler approach. Most people who try this sauce find out they have a higher tolerance for spice than they thought. It is perfect in **Dan Dan Noodles** (page 50).

1. HEAT a large saucepan over medium-high heat. Add:

   2 tablespoons neutral cooking oil

2. ADD when oil is shimmering:

   1 pound ground pork
   1 tablespoon soy sauce
   1½ teaspoons toasted sesame oil
   3 cloves garlic, minced
   1 tablespoon minced ginger
   1 teaspoon salt

3. COOK until the pork is no longer pink, about 10 minutes, stirring frequently and breaking the pork up with a wooden spoon. Deglaze the pan with:

   ¼ cup white wine

4. SCRAPE the bottom of the pan to release all the browned bits, then add:

   ½ cup unsweetened peanut butter
   ½ teaspoon ground Szechuan peppercorns (page 164)
   ¼ teaspoon ground white pepper
   1 teaspoon soy sauce
   3 tablespoons sugar or ¼ cup coconut nectar (page 169)
   2 tablespoons Spicy Miso Paste (page 128)
   ¼ cup douban chili paste (page 165)

5. COOK ingredients until aromatic, 1 to 2 minutes, stirring constantly. Stir in:

   2 cups chicken stock

6. BRING sauce just to a simmer and remove from heat.

USE CHICKEN OR BEEF
Feel free to use ground dark meat chicken or lean ground beef in place of the pork in this recipe.

YIELD: 5 CUPS

STORAGE: This sauce will keep in the refrigerator for up to 3 days.

DAN DAN NOODLES

Dan Dan noodles is a common Szechuan street dish that is typically prized for its spicy, smoky sauce. Our version is not as hot as the original. If you want more heat, drizzle on more Szechuan oil to finish.

1. KEEP warm:

   Spicy Szechuan Peanut Sauce (page 49)

2. BRING a big pot of water to a rolling boil and add:

   10   ounces dried udon noodles

3. COOK the noodles according to the package directions. Drain well and split between four bowls.

4. DIVIDE the peanut sauce between the bowls, then top each with:

   Pickled White Onions (page 142)
   Cilantro sprigs
   Pea shoots
   Szechuan Oil (page 158)

NOODLE ALTERNATIVE
If you find yourself pressed for time, we suggest pouring a cup of the sauce over a bowl of rice and then hitting it with all the toppings.

YIELD: 4 SERVINGS

MANCHAMANTELES SALSA

Manchamanteles, which translates to "tablecloth stainer," is a gloriously messy everything-but-the-kitchen-sink style of Mexican stew that typically includes pork, turkey, pineapple, tomato, cinnamon, almonds, and lard. We opted to make a vegetarian salsa so anyone could enjoy it. It goes great on rice and beans, but we love it on our **Pork Carnitas Tacos** (page 54), where it stays true to its tablecloth-stainer roots!

1. HEAT a medium saucepan over medium heat. Add:
   - 3 tablespoons neutral cooking oil

2. ADD when oil is shimmering:
   - 1 small onion, diced

3. COOK onion, stirring frequently, until soft and translucent but not browned, 4 to 5 minutes. Add:
   - 1 clove garlic, minced

4. COOK garlic and onion until fragrant, 30 seconds. Add:
   - 2 tablespoons sugar or 3 tablespoons coconut nectar
   - ¼ teaspoon chipotle powder
   - Big pinch of cinnamon
   - Pinch of ground cloves
   - 3½ teaspoons salt

5. COOK ingredients until sugar is dissolved and bubbling, about 1 minute. Add:
   - 1 tablespoon distilled white vinegar

6. STIR the saucepan quickly, then stir in:
   - 1 cup canned whole tomatoes
   - 1 (8-ounce) can diced pineapple in juice

7. BRING salsa to a simmer and cook for 20 minutes, stirring occasionally and breaking up chunks with a wooden spoon. Set aside to cool.

8. TRANSFER cooled salsa to a blender, then add:
   - 1 tablespoon lime juice

9. BLEND salsa on high until smooth.

TACOS OR DIP

This versatile salsa goes with almost any type of taco. You could also swirl in a spoonful of Lime Shallot Crème Fraîche (page 130) and use it as a dip for corn chips.

YIELD: 2 CUPS

STORAGE: This salsa will keep in the refrigerator for up to 7 days.

PORK CARNITAS TACOS

These tacos are a hit — especially during dark, wintry nights. Carnitas are tailor-made for a multiuse electric cooker like the Instant Pot, which cooks the pork in half the time it takes to braise on the stovetop. The finished product browns up well under a broiler for that crispy texture you want from carnitas.

1. CUT into 2-inch cubes:
   - 2 pounds boneless pork shoulder

2. SEASON pork liberally with salt. Allow to rest in the refrigerator, covered, for at least 6 hours or overnight.

3. TURN the sauté function of a multicooker to medium, then add:
   - 2 tablespoons neutral cooking oil

4. COOK the pork in batches when the oil is shimmering. Add a single layer of pork, being sure not to crowd the meat, and brown, 2 to 3 minutes per side. Transfer cooked pork to a plate, then repeat with the remaining pork, adding more oil as needed. Remove all meat from the cooker.

5. ADD to the cooker:
   - 1 yellow onion, finely diced
   - 2 cloves garlic, minced

6. COOK onion and garlic, stirring frequently, until the onion turns translucent and smells sweet, about 5 minutes, then add:
   - ½ cup water

7. SCRAPE all the brown bits at the bottom of the pot. Return the pork to the cooker, then add:
   - 1 teaspoon chili powder
   - 1 teaspoon ground coriander
   - 1 teaspoon ground cumin
   - 1 tablespoon lime juice
   - ¼ cup water
   - 2 tablespoons chopped cilantro

INSTANT POT RECIPE

YIELD: 6 SERVINGS

8. COVER the cooker and cook on high pressure for 1 hour, then allow the pressure to release naturally.

9. HEAT your oven's broiler to high. Transfer the carnitas to a rimmed baking sheet, then broil until the meat is crisp and lightly caramelized, 2 to 3 minutes.

10. HEAT on the grill or skillet:

   12 6-inch corn tortillas

11. DIVIDE tortillas among four plates and top each tortilla with:

   Carnitas

   2 teaspoons Manchamanteles Salsa (page 53)

   Pickled White Onions (page 142)

   Shredded cabbage

   Cilantro

   Squeeze of fresh lime juice

PULLED PORK SANDWICHES
If you have carnitas left over, make Asian pulled pork sandwiches with Hoisin Barbecue Sauce (page 66) and Seasoned Bean Sprouts (page 140)!

SCALLION GINGER JAM

As sauces go, this one is pretty versatile. You can spread it on sandwiches, spoon it over rice, or even use it on tacos. It is also visually striking — everyone who sees it on a dish will ask about it, especially when it's on **Clay Pot Miso Chicken** (page 58).

1. COMBINE in a medium bowl:

    2 bunches scallions, light green and white parts only, finely chopped
    1 teaspoon minced ginger
    1 teaspoon kosher salt
    ½ teaspoon sherry vinegar
    3 tablespoons neutral cooking oil

2. SET jam aside for at least 30 minutes before using.

LOX AND JAM

If you want to add some depth and complexity to a brunch standard, try replacing the red onions on a bagel with lox and cream cheese with scallion ginger jam. People will notice!

YIELD: ½ CUP

STORAGE: This jam will keep in the refrigerator for up to 4 days.

CLAY POT MISO CHICKEN

We love the sweet earthiness of this dish. It has a soothing depth that might take hours to achieve if not for the Instant Pot. This is one of those recipes that is more than the sum of its parts. The **Scallion Ginger Jam** (page 56) is a light and playful foil to this warm and hearty stew.

1. COMBINE in a large bowl:
    - 6 boneless, skinless chicken thighs
    - 2 teaspoons salt

2. TOSS the chicken and salt well to season evenly, then cover and refrigerate for at least 30 minutes.

3. TURN the sauté function of your multicooker to medium, then add:
    - 2 tablespoons neutral cooking oil

4. ADD when oil is shimmering:
    - 1 white onion, finely diced

5. COOK the onion until soft and beginning to brown, 5 to 7 minutes. Add:
    - 1½ tablespoons minced ginger
    - 1½ tablespoons minced garlic
    - ½ pound fresh shiitake mushrooms, stemmed and thinly sliced

6. COOK until the ginger and garlic are beginning to brown, 3 to 5 minutes. Add:
    - ½ cup water

7. SCRAPE all the brown bits from the bottom of the pot. Add:
    - ½ cup mirin (page 166)
    - 1 teaspoon lemon juice
    - 1 teaspoon apple cider vinegar

8. BOIL the sauce for 1 minute. Combine in a small bowl:
    - ½ cup white miso
    - 2 tablespoons soy sauce
    - 1 tablespoon honey

INSTANT POT RECIPE

YIELD: 4 SERVINGS

COOKINIG TIPS

Salt tenderizes meat and helps keep it moist and flavorful. If you have the time, we recommend salting your chicken at least 8 hours before you cook it. It will make a world of difference.

Where many braises taste better after they have sat overnight, this clay pot chicken works best when served right away.

9. ADD the miso mixture to the pot, then add the salted chicken thighs, and turn to evenly coat with the miso sauce. Cover and cook on high pressure for 13 minutes. Allow the pressure to release naturally.

10. REMOVE the lid and turn the sauté function to medium. Stir in:
    1 bunch mustard greens or curly green kale, ribs removed and coarsely chopped

11. COOK the chicken and greens for 5 minutes, stirring frequently. Divide the chicken and greens among four bowls, along with:
    4 cups cooked jasmine rice

12. GARNISH bowls with:
    Scallion Ginger Jam (page 56)
    Toasted sesame seeds

SHOYU RAMEN BROTH TARE

Good ramen starts with good broth, which has two components: stock made from bones and vegetables and stock made from fish and kelp (dashi). You cannot let the dashi boil, or it will be bitter. Good ramen also requires soy sauce seasoning, called tare, which you add just before serving the ramen. It helps to make the tare a day ahead, so that the flavors really come together.

We struggled for months with how to include a broth recipe in this book, as it normally takes at least 6 hours and requires a good deal of attention. It wasn't until we tried the Instant Pot that we were able to cut the time and labor down to something more manageable. This broth makes our **Coco Shoyu Ramen** (page 65) sing.

Make the Broth

1. COMBINE in your multicooker:
   - 1½ pounds chicken wings
   - 1½ pounds pork spare ribs
   - 1 bunch scallions, chopped
   - 1 large carrot, medium diced
   - 1 3-inch piece ginger, sliced into three pieces
   - 6 cloves garlic, halved
   - 10 cups cold water

2. COVER the cooker and cook on high pressure for 2 hours.

INSTANT POT RECIPE

YIELD: 12 CUPS

Recipe continues on page 62

BROTH

DASHI

TARE

Make the Dashi

3. COMBINE in a large pot while the broth is cooking:
   - 6 cups cold water
   - 1 ounce kombu (page 167)
   - 1½ cups bonito flakes (page 167)
   - ¼ cup dried scallops, chopped (page 167)
   - 1 tablespoon dried wakame (seaweed)

4. BRING dashi just to a simmer (do not allow to boil). Simmer for 20 minutes, then strain through a fine-mesh strainer. Set aside.

Finish the Broth and Add the Dashi

5. ALLOW the pressure of the multiuse cooker to release naturally when the broth is done cooking. Remove the lid and stir into the broth:
   - 2 cups bonito flakes
   - 1 bunch scallions, chopped

6. ALLOW broth to rest for 10 minutes, then strain through a fine-mesh strainer. Skim most (but not all) of the fat from the top of the broth.

7. STIR in the dashi.

STORAGE: The broth will keep in the refrigerator for up to 4 days or in the freezer for about 2 months.

Make the Shoyu Tare

8. COMBINE in a small saucepan:

   ¼ cup sake

   ¼ cup mirin (page 166)

9. SIMMER over medium heat for 3 minutes to cook off the alcohol. Then add:

   1 cup soy sauce

   1 2- by 8-inch piece kombu, broken into small pieces

   ¼ cup chopped dried scallops

   1½ cups bonito flakes, lightly packed

   2 teaspoons sugar

10. REDUCE the heat to low and allow to rest, without simmering, for 10 minutes. Remove from heat and cool to room temperature before straining through a fine-mesh strainer. (This will make about 1 cup of tare. It will keep in the refrigerator for at least 14 days, so save the leftover tare for a second round of ramen, or stir a couple of tablespoons into the Clay Pot Miso Chicken [page 58] when you add the stock.)

ROUND OUT SOUPS

Freeze leftover ramen broth in 1-cup containers and use it in soups and sauces that need extra umami.

COCO SHOYU RAMEN

The true beauty of a bowl of ramen is when a slew of ingredients come together to create something that is greater than the sum of its parts. The keys to producing excellent ramen at home are simple but very important. The tare and dashi are delicate, volatile ingredients and there are no shortcuts in their production and application. You must add the tare just before serving or it will lose some of its punch. Every part of this dish is important, so follow the recipe.

1. BRING a large pot of water to a rolling boil. Add:
   12 ounces ramen noodles, cooked according to package instructions

2. SET out four ramen bowls while the noodles are cooking. Add to each bowl:
   2 tablespoons Shoyu Tare
   1 teaspoon Togarashi Oil (page 156)
   1½ cups hot ramen broth

3. DIVIDE the cooked noodles among the bowls. Top each ramen bowl with:
   ½ cup cooked shredded chicken breast
   1 Soy-Cured Egg (page 136), cut in half
   2 tablespoons Pickled Shiitake Mushrooms (page 149)
   1 tablespoon scallion, thinly sliced
   4 squares toasted nori or 2 tablespoons Kizami nori (page 167)
   Chile Oil (page 154)

YIELD: 4 SERVINGS

DRY NOODLES
While we recommend using fresh ramen noodles, we understand that they can be tough to source if you aren't in a larger metropolitan area. Try using the dry noodles that come in a quality packet, like the ones you find at the natural foods store, instead of instant ramen noodles. We have had good results with Koyo brand organic ramen.

HOISIN BARBECUE SAUCE

We call this a grownup barbecue sauce. It has everything you want in a barbecue sauce — like the sweet, tangy aspects we all know and love — as well as a delicate floral note from the orange zest and a mild, aromatic spice from the curry. We particularly love it in **Hoisin-Glazed Baby Back Ribs** (page 68).

WHISK to combine in a large bowl:

- 1 cup ketchup
- ¾ cup hoisin sauce (purchased)
- ½ cup honey
- 5 tablespoons soy sauce
- 5 tablespoons white wine
- 5 tablespoons Seasoned Rice Wine Vinegar (page 157)
- ¼ cup toasted sesame seeds
- 3 tablespoons madras curry powder
- 3 tablespoons toasted sesame oil
- Zest of 2 oranges, grated
- 2 tablespoons minced garlic
- ¼ cup sambal oelek (page 165)

STIR-FRIES

Hoisin sauce is often used to flavor stir-fries, and you can use this barbecue sauce the same way to lend complex flavor. It also works well on grilled chicken and pairs nicely with Scallion Ginger Jam (page 56).

YIELD: 4 CUPS

STORAGE: The sauce will keep in the refrigerator for up to 14 days.

HOISIN-GLAZED BABY BACK RIBS

We are always trying to find a way to play ingredients off of one another, and this recipe is a shining success. The fatty, fruity ribs contrast beautifully with the brightness of the zesty slaw, and the mellow backdrop of the sushi rice works perfectly. We're also fans of this dish because if you cook the ribs in the Instant Pot the day before and make the slaw ahead of time, you can have dinner on the table in the amount of time it takes to cook the rice!

1. ADD to a large bowl:

   4 pounds baby back ribs, cut into chunks of 2 or 3 ribs, depending on rib size

2. GENTLY toss the ribs with:

   1 tablespoon salt

   1 cup Hoisin Barbecue Sauce (page 66)

   ½ cup water

3. ARRANGE the ribs standing up along the outer edge of the multiuse cooker insert, meat side facing out. Pour any sauce remaining in the bowl over the ribs, cover, and cook on high pressure for 32 minutes. Allow the pressure to release naturally. Discard the cooking liquid as it will be very fatty.

4. HEAT your oven's broiler to high. Transfer the ribs, meat side down, to a rimmed baking sheet, then brush the ribs with:

   ½ cup Hoisin Barbecue Sauce

5. BROIL the ribs until they are charred in spots, 2 to 4 minutes. Flip them over, then brush on:

   ½ cup Hoisin Barbecue Sauce

6. CONTINUE to broil the ribs until well caramelized and slightly charred, 2 to 4 minutes.

7. SET out four bowls, and add to each:

   1 cup cooked sushi rice

   Zesty Jalapeño Cabbage Slaw (page 44)

   ¼ of the hoisin-glazed baby back ribs

   1 tablespoon toasted sesame seeds

NOTE ON GRILLING

It is important to note that your ribs are already cooked before they touch the grill! We use the grill to reheat the ribs before serving and to impart flavor as you brush on the sauce and develop a nice glaze. The grill doesn't have to be terribly hot for this process; in fact, low and slow is the way to go to caramelize some of the sugars in the sauce.

INSTANT POT RECIPE

YIELD: 4 SERVINGS

PLUM SAUCE

When you order mu shu at a Chinese restaurant, they serve it with hoisin sauce. More often than not, it is dark, thick, and straight from a jar. We wanted to celebrate the intensity that has made hoisin sauce, and mu shu, so popular while cutting some of the more oppressive notes. We accomplished this by adding plum and oyster sauce until we really couldn't call it hoisin sauce anymore! Use it to make the **East-West Rice Bowl** (page 72) or as a dipping sauce for fresh spring rolls filled with fresh mango and mint.

1. COMBINE in a food processor:
   - ½ cup plum sauce
   - ½ cup hoisin sauce
   - ¼ cup oyster sauce
   - 1 tablespoon sambal oelek (page 165)
   - 1½ tablespoons water
   - 1 clove garlic, minced
   - 1 scallion, finely chopped

2. PROCESS ingredients until well combined. With machine still running, slowly drizzle in:
   - ¼ cup neutral cooking oil
   - 1 teaspoon toasted sesame oil

3. CONTINUE processing sauce until thick and smooth, stopping to scrape down sides as necessary.

VEGETARIAN

To make this vegetarian, just omit the oyster sauce. Substitute tofu cubes for the chicken in the rice bowl.

YIELD: 2 CUPS

STORAGE: The sauce will keep in the refrigerator for up to 14 days.

EAST-WEST RICE BOWL

At its core, this is really just a big bowl of mu shu chicken served over rice, but that doesn't do it justice. The plum sauce takes this to another place. It reminds us of all the mu shu we've ever had, but the flavors are never overpowering or heavy feeling.

1. HEAT a large skillet over medium-high heat, and add:
   - 1 tablespoon neutral cooking oil

2. ADD when oil is shimmering:
   - 1 tablespoon finely chopped garlic
   - 2 teaspoons finely chopped ginger

3. COOK garlic and ginger until aromatic, stirring constantly, 30 seconds. Add:
   - 1 carrot, peeled and cut into matchsticks
   - 1 large head bok choy, sliced crosswise into 1-inch pieces
   - 1 cup bean sprouts
   - 2 chicken breasts, cooked and cut into 1-inch cubes (about 3 cups)

4. INCREASE heat to high and sauté mixture, tossing frequently, until vegetables are lightly caramelized but still crunchy, 4 to 5 minutes. Remove from heat, then add:
   - 1 tablespoon toasted sesame oil
   - 2 teaspoons kosher salt

5. TOSS vegetable and chicken mixture once or twice to combine, then set aside.

6. DIVIDE among four bowls:
   - 4 cups cooked jasmine rice
     Sautéed vegetables and chicken
   - 1 cup Plum Sauce (page 71)
   - 4 scallions, sliced
   - 4 teaspoons toasted sesame seeds

OTHER INCARNATIONS
This recipe presents as a rice bowl, but over the last 20 years we've used a number of different approaches. You could wrap it in tortillas and serve as burritos or combine it with any type of Indian flatbread like paratha or roti.

YIELD: 4 SERVINGS

KOREAN HOT PEPPER SAUCE

Every cuisine seems to have a quintessential table sauce — something sweet and tangy that is always available to jazz up dinner. Ketchup, Sriracha, and nuoc cham (Vietnamese dipping sauce made from fish sauce) all come to mind. This is our version of Korea's ubiquitous funky, spicy, and sweet table sauce. We use it in lettuce wraps, **Grilled Short Rib Tacos** (page 76), and one of its most popular showcases: **Bibimbap** (page 78).

WHISK together in large bowl:

- 1 cup gochujang (page 165)
- ½ cup sugar or mild honey
- ½ cup hot water
- 1 teaspoon apple cider vinegar
- 1 teaspoon toasted sesame oil
- 1½ teaspoons toasted sesame seeds
- 1½ teaspoons tamari
- 1 teaspoon neutral cooking oil

WING IT

We first developed this sauce to make spicy Korean wings, and they remain a staff meal favorite at Coco. If you would like to try it out, just toss the cooked wings in a mixing bowl with some sauce and a little bit of honey right after the wings come out of the fryer or oven.

YIELD: 2 CUPS

STORAGE: The sauce will keep in the refrigerator for up to 14 days.

GRILLED SHORT RIB TACOS

Tacos like these have been wildly popular at food trucks around the country for years, probably because the flavor profiles of Korean and Mexican food have so much in common. You can go into any Korean restaurant and order grilled short ribs and wrap them in lettuce leaves; the tortillas just make an already fantastic meal a little more substantial.

1. COMBINE in a large bowl:

    1½ pounds ¼-inch-thick flanken-style short ribs (see note)
    Kalbi Marinade (page 134)

2. COAT the ribs well, then marinate in the refrigerator for at least 2 hours and up to 24 hours.

3. TURN grill on high. While waiting for it to preheat, place in a medium bowl:

    ½ small head green cabbage, finely shredded
    2 tablespoons Seasoned Rice Wine Vinegar (page 157)
    2 teaspoons toasted sesame oil
    2 teaspoons kosher salt

4. TOSS gently to combine and set aside. Prepare and set aside other garnishes:

    1 cup cilantro, chopped
    2 limes, cut into wedges
    Scallion Ginger Jam (page 56)
    Korean Hot Pepper Sauce (page 74)

5. COOK ribs for 2 minutes on each side. Transfer to a large plate, and allow to cool enough to handle safely. Cut the meat off the bones, and chop into bite-sized pieces.

6. HEAT on the grill:

    12 6-inch corn or flour tortillas

7. DIVIDE tortillas among four plates. Spread each with a small spoonful of the scallion ginger jam, then add the short ribs and 2 teaspoons of the Korean hot pepper sauce or to taste. Top with seasoned cabbage, cilantro, and toasted sesame seeds. Serve with lime wedges.

COOKING TIPS

We like to marinate meat in a large ziplock bag. Add the meat, pour in the marinade, squeeze out the air, and seal it up. This ensures an even coating and reduces the chances of cross-contamination.

Grill and chop the short ribs about half an hour ahead of time, then leave them in a skillet on the stove so you can quickly reheat them just before serving.

YIELD: 4 SERVINGS

NOTE:
Flanken-style short ribs are thinly sliced across the bone so each slice contains some of the rib bone.

BIBIMBAP

Bibimbap is an open book in Korean comfort food. As long as you have some rice and some things to stir into it, you can take it wherever you like. We like bibimbap because it can be both visually stunning and delicious, and you can prepare everything ahead of time and assemble it at your leisure. Start with a couple of spoonfuls of the **Korean Hot Pepper Sauce** (page 74) and mix everything together well, then add more sauce to taste.

1. DIVIDE among four bowls:
   - 4 cups cooked sushi rice
   - 1 cup Xander's Cucumber Pickles (page 146)
   - 1 cup Quick Kimchi (page 145)
   - 2 cups Seasoned Bean Sprouts (page 140)
   - 2 cups Seasoned Carrots (page 140)
   - ½ cup Pickled Shiitake Mushrooms (page 149)
   - Grilled Short Ribs (page 76), deboned and cut into bite-size pieces
   - 4 Soy-Cured Eggs (page 136), cut in halves

2. SERVE with:
   - Korean Hot Pepper Sauce

3. GARNISH with:
   - Toasted sesame seeds

WRAP IT UP

Try wrapping up your bibimbap. We like to stir everything up and then scoop it into a lettuce leaf, almost like a taco.

Toasted nori (the snack from the grocery store works great) is another simple addition.

YIELD: 4 SERVINGS

THAI PEANUT SAUCE

When we tell people we are working on a cookbook, the first question from them is invariably, "Will the peanut sauce be in there?" We've come to terms with the popularity of this sauce, which is easy when the final product is as addictive as this one. Most peanut sauces are thick and heavy, and we've managed to thin out this one — but not water it down — with coconut milk. We love it in our **Thai Chicken Rice Bowl** (page 82).

1. MELT in a medium saucepan over medium heat:
   - 2 tablespoons light brown sugar
   - 2 tablespoons mild honey

2. ADD:
   - 7 tablespoons unsweetened peanut butter
   - 2 tablespoons red Thai curry paste

3. WHISK constantly until peanut butter and curry paste are fully incorporated. Add:
   - 1 (13.5-ounce) can coconut milk
   - 1 teaspoon lime juice
   - ½ teaspoon salt
   - 2 tablespoons hoisin sauce (purchased)

4. CONTINUE whisking until all ingredients are melted and just combined.

VERSATILE SAUCE

There is no shortage of places to use peanut sauce. Our favorites include as an accompaniment to grilled chicken satay, or if you are feeling brave, with Gado Gado — an Indonesian mixed vegetable salad.

YIELD: 2¼ CUPS

STORAGE: The sauce will keep in the refrigerator for up to 4 days.

THAI CHICKEN RICE BOWL

Unmi often says that her gravestone will read "Here Lies the Thai Chicken Lady," and it is not clear whether she is joking. This dish has stayed in rotation for years because when you mix rice, peanut sauce, and Thai slaw together, magical things happen.

DIVIDE among four bowls:

4	cups cooked jasmine rice
2	cups cooked and cubed chicken breast
1	cup Thai Peanut Sauce (page 81)
2	cups Thai Cabbage (page 133)
1	cup chopped romaine lettuce
¼	red onion, thinly sliced
¼	cup chopped mint

YIELD: 4 SERVINGS

KOREAN BOLOGNESE

We developed this meat sauce as a way to introduce people to some of the more common Korean flavors. This sauce is sweet and spicy and unmistakably Korean, and when you pour it over **Korean Spaghetti** (page 86) or stuff it in **Korean Sloppy Joes** (page 88), you'll have no trouble getting people to try it.

1. HEAT in a large saucepan over medium heat:
   - 2 tablespoons neutral cooking oil

2. ADD when oil begins to shimmer:
   - ½ yellow onion, finely chopped

3. SAUTÉ onion until translucent but not beginning to brown, about 5 minutes. Add:
   - 1 tablespoon minced ginger
   - 4 cloves garlic, minced

4. COOK ginger and garlic until aromatic, about 1 minute. Increase heat to medium-high and add:
   - 1 pound ground pork

5. COOK mixture until the pork is no longer pink, about 10 minutes, stirring frequently and breaking up the pork with a wooden spoon.

6. DEGLAZE the pan with:
   - ¼ cup white wine

7. SCRAPE the bottom of the pan to release all the browned bits, then add:
   - ¼ cup tomato paste
   - 2 tablespoons Spicy Miso Paste (page 128)
   - 1 tablespoon gochujang (page 165)
   - ½ cup Korean Hot Pepper Sauce (page 74)
   - 2 cups chicken stock
   - 1 tablespoon mild honey
   - ½ teaspoon salt
   - 1 teaspoon soy sauce
   - 2 teaspoons Seasoned Rice Wine Vinegar (page 157)

8. SIMMER sauce for 20 minutes, until slightly reduced but still fairly loose.

MAKE IT MILDER

If you are worried about spiciness, omit the gochujang (there is some in the hot pepper sauce already).

YIELD: 4 CUPS

STORAGE: The sauce will keep in the refrigerator for up to 3 days or in the freezer for up to 1 month.

KOREAN SPAGHETTI

We've always found it odd that it took so long for Korean food to catch on with the American palate because it has so much that Americans love — like beef barbecue, or in this case, pork barbecue. This dish looks like spaghetti and meat sauce, but when people taste it, a whole new world opens up to them. It's particularly a hit with kids.

1. KEEP warm:
   4 cups Korean Bolognese (page 85)

2. COOK according to package instructions:
   10 ounces dried spaghetti

3. DRAIN spaghetti well, and then transfer to a large bowl.
   Add to the bowl:
   1 tablespoon cold butter
   ¼ cup Scallion Ginger Jam (page 56)

4. TOSS spaghetti and jam well to combine, then divide among four bowls. Top each bowl with 1 cup of the Bolognese, then add:
   Pinch of toasted sesame seeds

YIELD: 4 SERVINGS

KOREAN SLOPPY JOES

This is a perfect use for any leftover Korean Bolognese, and it is a strong enough recipe to merit making the sauce just for this application. Just remember to let the sauce reduce to a thicker consistency so that it will stay in the sandwich without making the bread too soggy.

1. HEAT in a saucepan over medium heat:

   3 cups Korean Bolognese (page 85)

2. REDUCE the sauce to a thick consistency, 20 to 30 minutes. Slice and toast:

   4 large hamburger buns or brioche rolls

3. SPREAD on each roll:

   Mayonnaise or mustard

4. DIVIDE the Bolognese and place it onto the buns. Serve with:

   Pickled White Onions (page 142)

KOREAN SIDES
We really can't eat a sandwich like this without pickles and potato chips. Why not go Korean and use toasted nori chips and our Quick Kimchi (page 145) instead?

YIELD: 4 SERVINGS

CHOW FUN SAUCE

This recipe is shockingly simple and yields a rich, umami-packed broth that is still delicate enough to be served with fresh rice noodles in **Coriander Shrimp Chow Fun** (page 92). This is another family meal favorite.

1. STIR to combine in a small bowl, then set aside:
     1 tablespoon cornstarch
     1 tablespoon cold water

2. WHISK to combine in a medium saucepan over medium heat:
     ¼ cup oyster sauce (page 165)
     ½ cup soy sauce
     ½ cup water
     ¼ cup sugar or coconut nectar
     ¾ teaspoon toasted sesame oil
     3 tablespoons chicken stock

3. BRING sauce to a simmer, then slowly drizzle in the cornstarch slurry, whisking constantly. Simmer for 1 minute to fully activate the starch.

OTHER USES

The great thing about this sauce is that it isn't just for noodles. In a pinch, we'll use rice instead and finish it with Scallion Ginger Jam (page 56). We also use it on any type of fish.

YIELD: 1½ CUPS

STORAGE: The sauce will keep in the refrigerator for up to 4 days.

CORIANDER SHRIMP CHOW FUN

The ingredients in this dish are all pretty typical for a Chinese stir-fry, but we wanted to avoid the muddiness of flavor and presentation that can result from tossing a whole bunch of stuff together with some soy sauce. This dish is much crisper and cleaner than a typical stir-fry and really pops when you set it in front of someone.

1. PREHEAT the oven to 200°F/90°C. Place a large pot of water over high heat.

2. TOSS to combine in a large bowl while the water heats:
   - 1   pound Gulf shrimp (see note), peeled and cleaned
   - 2   tablespoons ground coriander
   - 2   teaspoons salt

3. HEAT a large skillet over high heat and add:
   - 2   tablespoons neutral cooking oil

4. ADD the shrimp when you see the first wisps of smoke starting to rise from the pan. Cook, tossing frequently, until shrimp are just cooked through, 3 to 4 minutes. Remove shrimp to an ovenproof platter, cover lightly with aluminum foil, and place in the oven to keep warm.

5. ADD to the water when it is boiling:
   - 10   ounces wide rice noodles

6. COOK noodles according to package instructions and drain well. Divide the noodles and the shrimp among four bowls. Add to each bowl:
   - ½   cup Chow Fun Sauce (page 91)
   - 2   teaspoons Szechuan Oil (page 158)
   - ½   cup pea shoots

COOKING TIP

To add a crisp texture and nice flavor to the shrimp, dust with crushed coriander before cooking. It also helps keep the shrimp from sticking to the pan.

NOTE:

There are plenty of shrimp on the market from dubious sources, so we look for Gulf shrimp. You can always start a dialogue with your fishmonger to help you source healthy and sustainable shrimp.

YIELD: 4 SERVINGS

GENERAL TSO'S SAUCE

Unmi decided to try making General Tso's Sauce without ever having tried what it was "supposed" to be (overbearingly sweet and thick). Thus, she created something that really lets the best shine through. This is a bold, bright, and vibrant take on one of America's most ubiquitous guilty pleasures. We use this sauce in **General Tso's Tofu** (page 96), but don't be afraid to use it with chicken or shrimp. We also like to lightly dress roasted Brussels sprouts with it and serve as a side dish.

1. COMBINE in a blender:
   - 1 1½-inch piece ginger, sliced
   - 2 cloves garlic, sliced
   - 1½ tablespoons cornstarch
   - ½ cup kecap manis (sweet soy sauce) (page 165)
   - ½ cup soy sauce
   - 2 tablespoons sugar
   - 2 tablespoons distilled white vinegar
   - 2 tablespoons Seasoned Rice Wine Vinegar (page 157)
   - ¼ cup white wine
   - 1½ teaspoons toasted sesame oil
   - ¼ teaspoon red pepper flakes

2. BLEND on low to start, then slowly turn up to high and blend until no large pieces of ginger or garlic remain, about 20 seconds.

3. HEAT in a medium saucepan over medium heat:
   - 2 tablespoons neutral cooking oil

4. POUR sauce into pan when oil is shimmering. Bring sauce to a simmer, stirring frequently. Simmer for 1 minute to fully activate the cornstarch.

SWEET ALTERNATIVE
You can replace the kecap manis and sugar with ½ cup coconut nectar.

YIELD: 1½ CUPS

STORAGE: The sauce will keep in the refrigerator for up to 7 days.

GENERAL TSO'S TOFU

The crispiness of the tofu is what sets this recipe apart. In order to retain that slight crunch, we recommend coating the tofu with the sauce just before serving it!

1. CUT into 16 cubes:
   - 1 pound drained extra-firm tofu

2. SEASON tofu with:
   - Salt

3. PLACE in a large bowl:
   - 2 cups panko

4. PLACE in a second large bowl:
   - 3 large egg whites
   - 3 tablespoons cornstarch

5. WHISK egg whites and cornstarch until cornstarch is fully dissolved and mixture is smooth. Add tofu and stir gently to coat. Remove tofu with a slotted spoon, allowing excess egg white mix to drain off, then place in the bowl with panko. Toss gently to coat evenly.

6. HEAT to 375°F/190°C in a large, deep saucepan or Dutch oven (see note):
   - 4 cups neutral cooking oil

7. ADD the tofu, working in batches if necessary to prevent overcrowding, and fry until crispy and golden brown, 5 minutes, flipping halfway through. Remove tofu with a slotted spoon and drain on paper towels.

8. PLACE drained tofu in a large bowl, and toss with:
   - 1 cup General Tso's Sauce (page 95) (heated)

9. DIVIDE the tofu among four bowls, and add to each bowl:
   - ½ cup cooked sushi rice
   - ½ cup Broccoli Salad (page 40)
   - 1 tablespoon toasted, chopped cashews

NOTE:
Use a candy or deep-fry thermometer to ensure proper temperature. If you don't have one, the oil is ready when it looks wavy and a piece of bread sizzles instantly when dropped into it.

YIELD: 4 SERVINGS

VEGAN COCONUT CURRY

COCONUT CREAM

A Thai curry is only as good as the coconut milk you use in it. It needs to be sweet and full-bodied and contain a lot of the coconut cream that adds thickness and texture. You really need to use a rubber spatula to get all the thicker coconut cream out of the can, as it will want to stick to the sides.

NOTE:
Check the label on the curry paste, as many contain fish or shellfish products. Mae Ploy and Thai Kitchen brands tend to be vegan.

YIELD: 4½ CUPS

STORAGE: The sauce will keep in the refrigerator for up to 7 days.

The secret to this curry's success lies in how it has multiple layers of heat, with none of them being overwhelming. That complex spiciness is balanced by the floral notes of the vadouvan curry and then rounded out by palm sugar and coconut oil. Palm sugar is hard to replace in this recipe; it can be sourced easily online or at your local Asian market. We love how three different cuisines (Indian, Thai, and Korean) cooperate so well in this sauce, lending delicious harmony to the **Steamed Kabocha Squash and Tofu Rice Bowl** (page 100).

1. COMBINE in a small food processor:
   - 5 cloves garlic, chopped
   - 2 tablespoons chopped ginger
   - 2 shallots, chopped
   - ¼ cup chopped onion
   - 2 teaspoons neutral cooking oil

2. PULSE ingredients until very finely chopped and resembling a paste. Place a large saucepan over medium-high heat, and add:
   - 2 tablespoons coconut oil

3. ADD the garlic/ginger paste when the oil starts to shimmer, and cook, stirring and scraping frequently, until golden brown, 5 to 10 minutes. Add:
   - 1–2 teaspoons red Thai curry paste (see note)
   - 1 tablespoon gochujang (page 165)
   - 2 tablespoons vadouvan curry powder (page 164)
   - ½ cup canned whole tomatoes

4. BRING ingredients to a simmer and cook, stirring and breaking up tomatoes until jamlike, about 5 minutes. Add:
   - 2 (13.5-ounce) cans coconut milk
   - 1½ cups coconut water, without pulp
   - 3 tablespoons chopped palm sugar (page 169) or 2 tablespoons mild honey
   - 1 tablespoon tamari
   - 4 kaffir lime leaves
   - 2 star anise pods

5. BRING curry just to a simmer, and then cook for 20 minutes. Remove from the heat and allow to cool. Strain out the lime leaves and star anise, and adjust salt to taste if needed. Finish with:
   - Very small pinch of cinnamon

STEAMED KABOCHA SQUASH AND TOFU RICE BOWL

The kabocha provides a mellow sweetness that works very well in this recipe, but in a pinch, you can substitute butternut squash. If you prefer a different protein, the coriander shrimp from page 92 is fantastic in this.

1. CUT in half:
    1 kabocha squash

2. SCOOP out the seeds and discard, then cut each squash half into 1-inch-wide wedges. Steam squash in a vegetable steamer for 15 minutes. Allow squash to cool enough to handle safely, remove skin if desired, and cut into 1-inch cubes.

3. PLACE squash in a large bowl and add:
    2 teaspoons coconut oil
    Pinch of salt

4. TOSS squash gently until well combined and set aside.
    Heat in a large saucepan:
    4½ cups Vegan Coconut Curry (page 99)

5. ADD the kabocha squash to the curry, then add:
    1 (12-ounce) package silken tofu, cut into 1-inch cubes

6. DIVIDE the curry among four bowls, then garnish with:
    Chopped cilantro
    Chopped mint
    Ginger Oil (page 152)

7. SERVE the curry with steamed rice.

TURN IT INTO SOUP!
You can also turn the coconut curry into a noodle soup: add 1 more cup of coconut water to the curry, and leave out the tofu and squash. Add cooked rice noodles to the curry just before serving so that the noodles don't absorb most of the broth.

YIELD: 4 SERVINGS

CILANTRO SALSA VERDE

Salsa verde is a versatile sauce that we use frequently, most especially in **Chili Con Carne** (page 104). There are many iterations, but the goal is always to balance the aromatic herbs, pungent garlic, and fruity olive oil with the bright and tangy macerated shallots. You can round it out even further by adding chopped olives or pounded anchovies for umami.

1. COMBINE in a small bowl:
   - 1 shallot, finely chopped
   - 1 tablespoon lime juice
   - Pinch of kosher salt

2. ALLOW the shallots to macerate for 20 minutes. Meanwhile, stir to combine in a medium bowl:
   - ¼ cup finely chopped cilantro
   - 1 small clove garlic, pounded
   - ¼ cup olive oil
   - ¼ teaspoon kosher salt

3. STRAIN the shallots, reserving the lime juice. Add the shallots to the cilantro mixture, along with 1 teaspoon of the reserved lime juice. Stir well to combine.

OTHER USES

This salsa verde goes well with grilled fish or chicken. Add some toasted sliced almonds for extra crunch.

YIELD: ¾ CUP

STORAGE: The salsa will keep in the refrigerator for up to 1 day.

CHILI CON CARNE

This is our daughter's favorite dish, and she pretty much insisted on its inclusion in this book. Luckily, it happens to be an incredibly simple and tasty dinner. We like to serve this chili with lime wedges and lots of corn chips! Nachos whipped up in a toaster oven also work well.

1. PLACE a large skillet or Dutch oven over medium heat, and add:
    - 2 tablespoons neutral cooking oil

2. ADD when oil is shimmering:
    - 1 yellow onion, finely chopped
    - 3 cloves garlic, minced

3. COOK until onions are translucent and soft, 5 minutes, stirring frequently. Add:
    - 1 pound ground beef
    - 2 tablespoons chili powder
    - 1 teaspoon kosher salt

4. INCREASE heat to medium-high and cook until ground beef is no longer pink, stirring frequently and breaking up meat with a wooden spoon, about 5 minutes. Add:
    - 1 (28-ounce) can diced fire-roasted tomatoes
    - 1 (15-ounce) can black beans, drained
    - 2 cups chicken stock
    - 2 cups fresh or frozen sweet corn
    - Zest of 1 lime

5. BRING chili just to a simmer, and then cook for 20 minutes. Stir in:
    - 1 tablespoon masa harina (page 169)
    - 1 teaspoon kosher salt

6. SIMMER chili for 5 minutes longer.

7. DIVIDE chili among four bowls. Top with:
    - 1 tablespoon Cilantro Salsa Verde (page 103)
    - Pickled White Onions (page 142)
    - Lime Shallot Crème Fraîche (page 130)

TACO NIGHT

Make tacos by cooking the chili longer to thicken, then putting the filling in taco shells and adding pickled white onions, cilantro salsa verde, and some shaved cabbage.

YIELD: 4 SERVINGS

GREEN THAI CURRY

Many green Thai curries are dominated by chile and fish flavors. We set out to make this one stand apart by emphasizing the perfumed notes of lemongrass and kaffir lime leaves and replacing the fish stock with coconut water so that the more floral and citrusy notes could shine through. It works brilliantly in our **Salmon and Green Thai Curry Rice Bowl** (page 108). Kaffir lime leaves are hard to find but well worth the search.

1. HEAT in a large saucepan over medium-high heat:
   - 1 tablespoon neutral cooking oil or coconut oil

2. ADD when oil is shimmering:
   - ½ white onion, diced
   - 1 small carrot, diced
   - 1 teaspoon salt

3. COOK vegetables until well caramelized, 5 to 10 minutes, stirring frequently. If vegetables start to stick to the bottom of the pan, add another teaspoon or two of oil. Add:
   - 3 tablespoons minced garlic
   - 2 tablespoons minced ginger
   - 1 large stalk lemongrass, finely chopped (about ¼ cup)
   - 3 kaffir lime leaves, finely chopped (or zest of 1 lime)

4. COOK mixture until fragrant and starting to brown, about 2 minutes. Add:
   - ½ cup chopped palm sugar (page 169)
   - 2 tablespoons green Thai curry paste

5. COOK mixture until sugar is bubbling and starting to caramelize, about 5 minutes. Add:
   - ¼ cup lime juice
   - ¼ cup fish sauce
   - 1 cup coconut water, without pulp
   - 3 (13.5-ounce) cans coconut milk

6. LOWER the heat and bring curry just to a simmer (do not allow the curry to boil or it will break). Simmer for 30 minutes. Allow to cool slightly, then strain out the solids.

THAI BURRITOS

For a thicker sauce, leave the solids in the curry and blend it. Put the sauce in a squirt bottle, cool it in the refrigerator so it gets even thicker, and use it for Thai salmon burritos (with some fresh cubed mango and mint).

YIELD: 4½ CUPS

STORAGE: The curry will keep in the refrigerator for up to 4 days.

SALMON AND GREEN THAI CURRY RICE BOWL

Around our house, a bowl of fresh rice, curry, and salmon is considered comfort food. It's a unique combination that we have for lunch or dinner, and the leftovers are one of our favorite breakfasts, too.

1. SEASON with salt:

   4   6-ounce skinned salmon fillets

2. HEAT a large skillet over medium-high heat, and add:

   2   tablespoons neutral cooking oil

3. ADD the salmon fillets, gently and skin side up, when oil is shimmering. Cook until golden brown, 4 to 5 minutes. Flip the fillets with a fish spatula, and continue cooking until fish feels firm to the touch, about 3 minutes longer. Remove pan from heat.

4. DIVIDE among four bowls:

   4   cups cooked jasmine rice
   4   cups Green Thai Curry (page 107)
       Cooked salmon fillets
   ½   cup Thai basil leaves or Italian basil

5. FINISH with:

   Chive Oil (page 154)

COOKING TIP

A nice pan (like a well-seasoned carbon-steel pan) and a fish spatula make a big difference when searing fish like salmon.

YIELD: 4 SERVINGS

PONZU

Japanese food is known for having a clean and minimal aesthetic, and ponzu is a great example of this philosophy. It has a delicate balance of wine, soy, ginger, and spice that really epitomizes the "less is more" mentality that makes Japanese cuisine so unique. We also adore how simple this is to make and how well it holds up for a few days. This sauce works well with delicate fish, like **Miso-Glazed Cod Rice Bowl** (page 112). Or add a couple of tablespoons of grated fresh daikon radish to make an exciting dipping sauce for tempura.

1. COMBINE in a small saucepan:
     1   cup mirin (page 166)
     1   1-inch piece ginger, sliced
     1½ teaspoons lime juice
     1½ teaspoons tamari (see note)
     ⅛   jalapeño, seeded if desired

2. SIMMER sauce for 5 minutes, and then strain.

NOTE:

It pays to be cautious with the tamari in this recipe, as too much can really throw the flavors out of whack. Remember that it is considerably easier to splash a little more tamari into the pot than it is to take some out.

YIELD: 1 CUP

STORAGE: The sauce will keep in the refrigerator for up to 7 days.

MISO-GLAZED COD RICE BOWL

There are more ways to overpower a delicate fish like cod than there are ways to showcase it. We found that the combination of miso marinade and ponzu succeeds in bringing out the sweet and elegant nature of the fish. We have been serving some iteration of this dish for years. Sometimes it's more polished and composed, and sometimes it's more relaxed and playful, like this.

1. COMBINE in a large bowl:
   - 1½ pounds black cod (sablefish), cut into four equal portions
   - 1 cup Miso Marinade (page 139)

2. COAT fish evenly with marinade, cover, then allow to marinate in the refrigerator for 30 minutes.

3. PREHEAT the oven to 400°F/200°C.

4. PLACE a large, ovenproof skillet over medium-high heat, and add:
   - 2 tablespoons neutral cooking oil

5. REMOVE the fish from the marinade, allowing excess to drip off. When the oil starts to shimmer, add the fish in a single layer. Cook until golden, 1 to 2 minutes. Flip each piece, then transfer the pan to the middle rack of the oven. Bake fish for 5 minutes or until fish is just cooked through and lightly caramelized.

6. SET out four bowls and add to each bowl:
   - 1 cup cooked sushi rice
   - Cooked miso-glazed cod fillet
   - ½ cup Pickled Japanese Turnips (page 150)
   - ¼ cup Ponzu (page 111)

7. GARNISH each bowl with:
   - Toasted sesame seeds
   - Ginger Oil (page 152)
   - Chive Oil (page 154)

COOKING TIP

The fish will caramelize very quickly from the mirin and sugar, so be careful not to burn the fish.

YIELD: 4 SERVINGS

TERIYAKI SAUCE

Before we developed our own teriyaki sauce recipe, we thought of all the words we would use to describe the typical teriyaki sauce. Words like syrupy, heavy, thick, and sweet came to mind. Then we set out to make a sauce that wasn't any of these things. We wanted something that complements food in our **Salmon Teriyaki Bento Box** (page 116) and doesn't make everything taste like soy and sugar. Mission accomplished.

1. COMBINE in a medium saucepan:
   - ½ cup soy sauce
   - ½ cup mirin (page 166)
   - ¼ cup sake
   - ¼ cup light brown sugar or ¼ cup mild honey
   - 2 small cloves garlic, smashed with the flat side of a knife
   - 2 1-inch slices ginger

2. BRING sauce just to a boil, reduce heat, and simmer for 10 minutes. Meanwhile, stir together in a small bowl:
   - 2 teaspoons cornstarch
   - 4 teaspoons cold water

3. STIR cornstarch slurry into the sauce, return to a simmer, and simmer 1 minute longer to fully activate the starch.

CHICKEN SKEWERS

We love this sauce as a glaze for grilled chicken and scallion skewers when we are in the mood for yakitori.

YIELD: 1½ CUPS

STORAGE: The sauce will keep in the refrigerator for up to 7 days.

SALMON TERIYAKI BENTO BOX

A bento box is a self-contained, single-serving Japanese meal. It is fun to make and just as fun to eat. We made bento boxes for Coco's ninth birthday, and they were a hit with the kids and the adults as well. You can fill the various compartments in a bento box with all sorts of things, so just use this recipe as a starting point for any number of possible dinners. Try kimchi and grilled short ribs, pickled shiitake mushrooms, or even **General Tso's Tofu** (page 96).

1. SEASON with salt:

    4   6-ounce skinned salmon fillets

2. HEAT a large skillet over medium-high heat, and add:

    2   tablespoons neutral cooking oil

3. ADD the salmon fillets, gently and skin side up, when oil is shimmering. Cook until golden brown, 4 to 5 minutes. Flip the fillets with a fish spatula, and continue cooking until the fish feels firm to the touch, about 3 minutes longer. Remove pan from heat.

4. DIVIDE among four bento boxes:

    Cooked salmon fillets

    2   cups Broccoli Salad (page 40)

    Seasoned Bean Sprouts (page 140)

    Seasoned Carrots (page 140)

    1   cup Xander's Cucumber Pickles (page 146)

    4   cups cooked sushi rice

    ½   cup Teriyaki Sauce (page 115)

BENTO BOX ARRANGEMENT
Use bento boxes with four large compartments for mains plus one small compartment for a sauce. We like to use one large compartment for protein, one for salad, one for pickles or rice, and one for seasoned vegetables.

YIELD: 4 SERVINGS

PHÆD THAI SAUCE

Our version of Phad Thai has all the flavors one would expect from this quintessential Thai noodle dish. We just switched the emphasis from the breathy notes of the fish sauce to the crisp citrus notes of the lime and tamarind. Using this sauce in **Shiitake Mushroom and Tofu Phad Thai** (page 119) is a way to introduce inexperienced palates to fish sauce without scaring them off.

1. COMBINE in a medium bowl:
    - ½ cup fish sauce
    - 4 teaspoons Seasoned Rice Wine Vinegar (page 157)
    - 7 tablespoons sugar or ½ cup coconut nectar (page 169)
    - 2 tablespoons plus 2 teaspoons sweet paprika (not smoked)
    - ½ cup tamarind juice (see sidebar)
    - 1 tablespoon lime juice
    - 3 cups hot water

2. STIR gently until the sugar has dissolved.

HOMEMADE TAMARIND JUICE
To make tamarind juice, add ½ cup tamarind paste to a bowl. Pour 2 cups of warm water over the paste and massage to separate the pulp from the seeds. Strain the mixture through a fine mesh strainer and reserve the liquid.

YIELD: 3½ CUPS

STORAGE: The sauce will keep in the refrigerator for up to 7 days.

SHIITAKE MUSHROOM AND TOFU PHAD THAI

Phad Thai is one of the most popular street foods in Thailand and is reflective of the climate and culture there. It is hot, sweet, funky, and completely captivating. Our version focuses on a cleaner, simpler sauce and a lighter, more delicate bite from the tofu and shiitake mushrooms.

1. PLACE in a large bowl:
    8   ounces medium-width rice noodles

2. ADD enough cold water to cover the noodles.
    Allow to soak for 45 minutes.

Recipe continues on next page

SHIITAKE MUSHROOM AND TOFU PHAD THAI *continued*

3. HEAT a wok or large skillet over high heat, and add:

    2 tablespoons neutral cooking oil

4. ADD when you see the first wisps of smoke starting to rise from the pan:

    2 tablespoons minced garlic

    1 red Thai chile, stemmed and minced or ⅛–¼ teaspoon red pepper flakes

    1 cup peeled and finely diced daikon radish

5. COOK the chile mixture for 1 minute, tossing frequently. Add:

    4 cups (7 ounces) stemmed and sliced shiitake mushrooms

    2 cups diced firm tofu

6. COOK tofu and mushroom mixture for 2 minutes, tossing frequently. Drain noodles, then add to the pan, along with:

    3 cups Phad Thai Sauce (page 118)

7. CONTINUE to cook noodle mixture and gently toss until most of the liquid is absorbed, about 5 minutes. Remove pan from the heat and stir in:

    ½ cup chopped roasted and salted peanuts

    2 cups mung bean sprouts

    4 scallions, sliced on the bias

    ½ cup chopped cilantro

8. DIVIDE the phad Thai between four bowls, and garnish with:

    Chopped peanuts

    Lime wedges

YIELD: 4 SERVINGS

MORNAY

Mornay is a classic French cheese sauce. It is the base for our **Macaroni and Cheese** (page 124) because it is tasty, sturdy, and versatile. We recommend Cabot's Sharp Cheddar.

1. COMBINE in a medium saucepan:
   - 3 cups milk
   - 1 cup heavy cream

2. HEAT over medium heat until fairly warm (about 100°F/38°C) but not too hot. Turn the heat off but leave the saucepan on the burner to keep the milk/cream mixture warm.

3. MELT in a large saucepan over medium heat:
   - 3 tablespoons unsalted butter

4. WHISK in once the butter is bubbling:
   - 3 tablespoons all-purpose flour

5. CONTINUE to whisk almost constantly until it is light tan, about 1 minute. Slowly whisk in the warm milk/cream mixture and continue to cook, whisking frequently and scraping the sides and bottom, until mixture thickens and comes to a slow simmer, 6 to 8 minutes longer.

6. ADD in three batches, whisking after each addition, until the cheese has almost melted:
   - 1 pound grated sharp cheddar cheese

7. REMOVE pan from heat and whisk, using residual heat to melt the cheese completely. Stir in:
   - 1½ teaspoons salt
   - ¼ teaspoon ground black pepper
   - ⅛–¼ teaspoon red pepper flakes
   - 2 teaspoons chopped fresh thyme
   - ¼ teaspoon Dijon mustard
   - Pinch of grated nutmeg

NOTE:
Don't worry if the Mornay seems loose; the pasta will absorb the liquid as it cools.

YIELD: 6 CUPS

MACARONI AND CHEESE

This macaroni and cheese recipe can stand on its own, but we love it because it can be used as a jumping off point for tons of exciting variations. We sometimes add roasted mushrooms to the mixture before we bake it, or if we want some spice, we will add roasted and chopped poblano peppers.

1. PREHEAT oven to 375°F/190°C. Place a rack in the middle of the oven.

2. BRING a large pot of well-salted water to a boil. Cook until just al dente:
   12 ounces elbow macaroni

3. DRAIN macaroni well and set macaroni aside in a large bowl.

4. POUR over macaroni and mix well:
   6 cups Mornay (page 122)

5. TRANSFER pasta to a 9- by 13-inch glass baking dish and set aside.

6. PLACE in a medium bowl:
   1 cup panko

7. MELT in a small saucepan:
   3 tablespoons unsalted butter

8. DRIZZLE the melted butter over the panko, tossing well to combine. Spread the panko over the top of the macaroni, and place in the preheated oven. Cook for 20 to 30 minutes or until the macaroni is bubbling and the panko is golden brown. Remove from the oven and allow to rest for 10 minutes before serving.

THE PERFECT SIDE
We love to serve macaroni and cheese with the Zesty Jalapeño Cabbage Slaw (page 44). The tangy, slightly spicy slaw is the perfect paring to balance this rich, cheesy baked pasta.

YIELD: 6 MAIN COURSE SERVINGS

CONDIMENTS, PICKLES, AND INFUSED OILS

PART 3

There is no better way to add spice, acidity, or texture to your daily food than to embrace the incredibly diverse world of pickles and condiments. And infused oils add a burst of color and flavor. While these recipes are relatively easy, they really can make the difference in many of the recipes in this book.

SPICY MISO PASTE

We refer to this paste as an umami bomb. It adds a potent depth to soups, sauces, and dressings that feature stronger, meatier flavors. Try it in **Spicy Szechuan Peanut Sauce** (page 49) or **Korean Bolognese** (page 85).

1. COMBINE in a blender:
   - ½ cup white miso
   - ½ cup red miso
   - ⅓ cup douban chili paste (page 165)
   - 1 small onion, diced
   - 6 cloves garlic, minced
   - 1 2-inch piece (1 ounce) ginger, diced
   - 3 tablespoons mirin (page 166)
   - 2 tablespoons neutral cooking oil
   - 1 tablespoon toasted sesame oil
   - 2 teaspoons sesame paste

2. PURÉE ingredients until very smooth.

3. TRANSFER paste to a medium saucepan, and simmer over medium heat for 5 minutes, stirring constantly.

YIELD: 2½ CUPS

STORAGE: The paste will keep in the refrigerator for up to 14 days.

LIME SHALOT CRÈME FRAÎCHE

We use this crème fraîche to finish all sorts of things, like **Chili Con Carne** (page 104), fish tacos, and stews and to top off baked potatoes.

1. COMBINE in a small bowl:

    1½ teaspoons finely chopped shallots

    2 tablespoons white wine vinegar

2. ALLOW shallots to macerate for 30 minutes. Strain, reserving vinegar.

3. COMBINE in a medium bowl:

    ½ cup crème fraîche

    1 teaspoon finely chopped chives

    Zest of ¼ lime

    ¼ teaspoon kosher salt

4. ADD strained shallots and ¼ teaspoon of the reserved vinegar to bowl. Allow to sit for 15 minutes. Stir and taste, adding a pinch more salt or vinegar if desired.

APPETIZERS

For a delicious hors d'oeuvre, we like to lightly simmer fingerling potatoes, let them cool, then peel and slice them lengthwise. We then top them with a dollop of the crème fraîche and a little sliced chive!

YIELD: ¾ CUP

STORAGE: The sauce will keep in the refrigerator for up to 2 days.

THAI CABBAGE

This Thai cabbage recipe is the secret weapon in the **Thai Chicken Rice Bowl** (page 82). You absolutely need it to succeed. Don't let that stop you from using it other places as well, such as the base for a salad or slipped into a taco.

1. COMBINE in a large bowl:
   - ¼ head green cabbage, finely shredded (4 cups)
   - ¼ head red cabbage, finely shredded (4 cups)
   - 1½ tablespoons salt

2. TOSS well, then set aside for 30 minutes. Transfer to a colander and rinse thoroughly with cold running water. Squeeze as much water from the cabbage as possible, and then transfer to a large bowl. Add:
   - 1 cup Thai sweet chili sauce (page 166)
   - 1 tablespoon Ginger Oil (page 152)

3. TOSS well to combine.

YIELD: 4 CUPS

STORAGE: The cabbage will keep in the refrigerator for up to 2 days.

KALBI MARINADE

This classic Korean marinade is mostly used for grilling meat. We use it for **Grilled Short Rib Tacos** (page 76), but this recipe would also be great with grilled chicken or pork.

COMBINE in a medium bowl:

- 1 kiwi, peeled and grated
- ¾ cup soy sauce
- 2 tablespoons sugar
- 2 tablespoons mild honey
- 2 tablespoons toasted sesame oil
- 5 small cloves garlic, minced
- 3 scallions, finely chopped
- 1 tablespoon toasted sesame seeds

YIELD: 1¼ CUPS

STORAGE: The marinade will keep in the refrigerator for up to 14 days.

SOY-CURED EGGS

A perfectly cooked soy-cured egg is one of our great simple pleasures. It looks like nothing else on the plate, and it adds a slightly sweet taste and unique texture to a bowl of **Coco Shoyu Ramen** (page 65) or **Bibimbap** (page 78).

1. BRING water to a boil in a medium saucepan and add:

   6 large eggs

2. BOIL eggs 8 minutes. Prepare an ice bath.

3. REMOVE eggs with a slotted spoon, transfer to the ice bath, and allow to cool completely.

4. COMBINE in a medium bowl:

   1 cup warm water

   1 cup soy sauce

   2 tablespoons sugar

   ¼ cup sherry vinegar

5. STIR marinade until sugar is dissolved and cool. When eggs are cool, peel them and place in the marinade. Refrigerate for at least 2 hours, or overnight, before using.

YIELD: 6 EGGS

STORAGE: The eggs will keep in the refrigerator for up to 2 days.

MISO MARINADE

This delicate and understated Japanese marinade is perfect for milder fish like cod, so we use it in our **Miso-Glazed Cod Rice Bowl** (page 112). We've also tossed roasted mushrooms and sweet potatoes in it and have been very happy with the results!

1. ADD to a small saucepan over medium heat:
   - ¾ cup mirin (page 166)
   - 2 cups white miso
   - 1¼ cups sugar

2. STIR and cook until the sugar has dissolved. Turn the heat off, then stir in until well combined:
   - ¼ cup sake

YIELD: 3 CUPS

STORAGE: The marinade will keep in the refrigerator for up to 14 days.

SEASONED BEAN SPROUTS

Beans sprouts add a refreshing taste and a light, crisp texture to our **Salmon Teriyaki Bento Box** (page 116), as well as to many Korean rice dishes, like **Bibimbap** (page 78). We usually eat half of them before we get to dinner, so we suggest making extra!

1. FILL a medium pot with water and bring to a rolling boil. Add:
   - 10 ounces fresh bean sprouts (4 cups)
2. COOK sprouts for 2 minutes. Remove with a slotted spoon to a bowl and let cool. Add to bowl:
   - 2 teaspoons toasted sesame oil
   - 2 teaspoons soy sauce
   - ½ teaspoon salt
3. STIR ingredients to combine.

YIELD: 2 CUPS

STORAGE: The bean sprouts will keep in the refrigerator for up to 3 days.

SEASONED CARROTS

Like the bean sprouts, these seasoned carrots are an important part of a good **Bibimbap** (page 78) and **Salmon Teriyaki Bento Box** (page 116).

1. FILL a medium pot with water and bring to a rolling boil. Add:
   - 2 large carrots, cut into matchsticks (2½ cups)
2. COOK carrots for 1 minute. Remove with a slotted spoon to a bowl and let cool. Add to bowl:
   - 1 teaspoon toasted sesame oil
   - 1 teaspoon soy sauce
   - ½ teaspoon salt
   - 1 teaspoon toasted sesame seeds
3. STIR ingredients to combine.

YIELD: 2 CUPS

STORAGE: The carrots will keep in the refrigerator for up to 3 days.

PICKLED WHITE ONIONS

These onions are a quick way to add extra brightness to all sorts of dishes, including our **Chili Con Carne** (page 104), **Korean Sloppy Joes** (page 88), and **Dan Dan Noodles** (page 50). We also like to add these pickles to our other sandwiches and salads for additional acid and texture!

1. BRING to a boil in a large nonreactive saucepan over high heat:
   - 3 cups water
   - 2 cups white wine vinegar
   - ¼ cup sugar or mild honey
   - 1 teaspoon whole coriander
   - 1 clove garlic, crushed
   - ¼ teaspoon red pepper flakes
   - 1 sprig thyme
   - ¼ teaspoon salt

2. PEEL while the brine heats:
   - 2 white onions

3. SLICE onions into ¼-inch rings, and place in a large heatproof bowl. When the brine comes to a boil, pour over the onions. Allow to cool to room temperature, then refrigerate. You can use the onions once they are cold.

TRY OTHER *ALLIUMS*
Sweet Vidalia onions and shallots are also good for pickling.

YIELD: 2 QUARTS

STORAGE: The onions will keep in the refrigerator for up to 7 days.

QUICK KIMCHI

There isn't a more Korean flavor than kimchi. That being said, it has a pretty intense flavor for inexperienced palates. Our version is slightly less pungent so it won't scare away any first-timers. It works beautifully in our **Bibimbap** (page 78).

1. CUT in half lengthwise and rinse well under running water:
   - 1 small head napa cabbage

2. DRY the cabbage and cut each half, lengthwise, into thirds. Cut the thirds into 1-inch pieces.

3. PLACE the cut cabbage in a large bowl and add:
   - 1½ tablespoons salt

4. COMBINE the cabbage and salt and stir until thoroughly combined. Set aside for 30 minutes.

5. MIX in a small bowl until uniform paste consistency:
   - 4 teaspoons salt
   - 4 cloves garlic, crushed
   - 2 tablespoons plus 2 teaspoons gochugaru (page 164)
   - 2 tablespoons sugar
   - 3 tablespoons plus 1 teaspoon Seasoned Rice Wine Vinegar (page 157)
   - 2 tablespoons plus 2 teaspoons toasted sesame oil
   - 2 tablespoons plus 2 teaspoons toasted sesame seeds

6. SQUEEZE and drain the salted cabbage of excess water. Add the paste to the cabbage and combine well. Cover and refrigerate for at least 30 minutes, or until chilled.

OTHER OPTIONS

Cucumbers and daikon radish make excellent quick kimchi.

YIELD: 4 CUPS

STORAGE: It will keep for at least 7 days in the refrigerator in an airtight container.

XANDER'S CUCUMBER PICKLES

When we asked one of our most trusted cooks, Xander, to create a foolproof quick pickle recipe, he approached it with the eye of a scientist and for several weeks there were containers of cucumbers in salt all over the place. The result was worth all of his hard work, as we use his recipe on a daily basis — whether in our **Chinese Chicken Salad** (page 36), **Bibimbap** (page 78), or **Salmon Teriyaki Bento Box** (page 116).

1. SLICE into ¼-inch rounds with a Japanese mandoline (see page 160) set to its widest setting, or a sharp knife:

   1 pound cucumbers, preferably Kirby or Persian

2. PLACE cucumbers in a large bowl, and toss with:

   2½ teaspoons salt
   4½ teaspoons sugar

3. ALLOW cucumbers to macerate at room temperature for 1 to 2 hours, stirring every 30 minutes. Refrigerate the pickles in their liquid until ready to use.

SCALE UP

If you have a kitchen scale and a calculator, you can scale this recipe to any size you need. Weigh the cucumber slices after cutting and toss with 2 percent of that weight in salt and 5 percent of that weight in sugar.

YIELD: 3 CUPS

STORAGE: The pickles will keep in the refrigerator for up to 7 days.

PICKLED SHIITAKE MUSHROOMS

These tangy, sweet mushrooms are packed with umami. They have one of the most unique flavors in this book and are essential for our **Coco Shoyu Ramen** (page 65). They are also delightful in **Bibimbap** (page 78).

1. PLACE in a medium heatproof bowl:

   2 ounces dried whole shiitake mushrooms

2. COVER mushrooms with boiling water, wrap the bowl tightly with plastic wrap, and let steep at room temperature until rehydrated, 1 hour.

3. DRAIN mushrooms, reserving 1 cup of the steeping liquid. Remove and discard stems, and then slice mushrooms into ¼-inch pieces.

4. COMBINE mushrooms and reserved liquid in a medium saucepan. Add:

   ½ cup sugar

   ½ cup sherry vinegar

   6 tablespoons soy sauce

   2 tablespoons water

   1 2-inch piece ginger, sliced into ½-inch rounds

5. SIMMER ingredients for 30 minutes, then remove from heat. Allow to cool to room temperature, then place in the refrigerator.

YIELD: 3 CUPS

STORAGE: Pickled mushrooms will keep in the refrigerator for up to 14 days.

PICKLED JAPANESE TURNIPS

We use lemon juice in this recipe to complement the sweet and floral notes of the turnips. They work beautifully in our **Miso-Glazed Cod Rice Bowl** (page 112).

1. **BRING** to a boil in a medium nonreactive saucepan:
   - 3 cups water
   - ¾ cup white wine vinegar
   - ¼ cup sugar
   - 2½ tablespoons salt
   - 1 teaspoon whole black peppercorns
   - 2 bay leaves

2. **REMOVE** brine from heat and allow to cool to room temperature. In a large bowl or lidded container, place:
   - 2 pounds Japanese turnips, peeled and wedged
   - 6 tablespoons lemon juice
   - Zest of 1 lemon

3. **POUR** the brine over the turnips, cover, and refrigerate overnight.

MEYER LEMONS
We like to use juice from Meyer lemons when we can find them. These lemons are less acidic and add beautiful aroma.

YIELD: 2 QUARTS

STORAGE: Pickles will keep in the refrigerator for up to 7 days.

PICKLED GINGER

We prefer to pickle our own ginger because most store-bought products are overly sweet and somewhat artificial tasting. We add this to our **Togarashi Dressing** (page 39), and it would be perfect for sushi.

1. THINLY slice:
   - 1   4-inch piece fresh ginger

2. PLACE ginger in a jar and set aside. Combine in a small saucepan over high heat:
   - ½   cup white wine vinegar
   - ½   cup water
   - 2   tablespoons sugar
   - 1   teaspoon salt

3. BRING brine to a boil, then reduce heat and simmer for 5 minutes. Pour hot brine over the ginger, and let cool. Cover and refrigerate overnight.

YOUNG GINGER
Fresh, young pink ginger makes the most delicate ginger pickles.

YIELD: 1 CUP

STORAGE: The pickled ginger will keep in the refrigerator for up to 14 days.

GINGER OIL

This is our subtlest oil. Its floral aroma and mild flavor round out salads, soups, and noodle dishes perfectly. We use it in our **Steamed Kabocha Squash and Tofu Rice Bowl** (page 100), **Miso-Glazed Cod Rice Bowl** (page 112), and **Thai Cabbage** (page 133).

1. COMBINE in a blender:
   - 2   cups thinly sliced ginger
   - 1⅓   cup neutral cooking oil

2. BLEND on high until puréed. Refrigerate overnight, and strain through a fine-mesh strainer.

YIELD: 1 CUP

STORAGE: The oil will keep for 7 days in the refrigerator.

Oils

Our ginger, chive, and chile oils are the simplest recipes in this book, but they can add depth of flavor and splashes of color to almost any dish. These are our secret weapons in the kitchen, and sometimes a little splash is all it takes to push a dish over the line from good to great.

CHIVE OIL

This is the most vivid oil we use on a daily basis, including in our **Miso-Glazed Cod Rice Bowl** (page 112). It has a grassy herbal flavor and a beautiful bright green color.

1. COMBINE in a blender:
   - ¾ cup (1 ounce) chopped chives
   - 1 cup neutral cooking oil
   - Pinch of salt

2. BLEND on high until puréed. Refrigerate overnight, then strain through a fine-mesh strainer.

YIELD: ¾ CUP

STORAGE: The oil will keep for 3 days.

CHILE OIL

The purpose of this oil is to provide a little background heat and just a hint of color. If it is too spicy for you, just add some more neutral cooking oil. It works well in **Coco Shoyu Ramen** (page 65).

1. COMBINE in a small saucepan:
   - 1 tablespoon red pepper flakes
   - 2 small cloves garlic, crushed
   - 1 tablespoon canned tomato, crushed
   - 1 tablespoon tomato sauce
   - Pinch of salt
   - 1 cup neutral cooking oil

2. BRING mixture just to a simmer, and remove from heat. Allow to rest at room temperature for 4 hours, and strain.

YIELD: 1 CUP

STORAGE: The oil will keep for 14 days.

TOGARASHI OIL

We can't stress enough how important it is to use Oaktown Spice Shop's Shichimi Togarashi blend here. Many other blends can come out bitter and metallic-tasting. We use this in **Korean Hot Pepper Dressing** (page 23), **Togarashi Dressing** (page 39), and **Coco Shoyu Ramen** (page 65).

1. COMBINE in a small saucepan:
   - 2 medium shallots, finely minced
   - 3 cloves garlic, finely minced
   - ¾ teaspoon toasted sesame seeds
     Pinch of salt
   - 1 cup neutral cooking oil

2. BRING ingredients to a simmer over medium-low heat, and cook until the garlic is crispy and light brown, 10 minutes. Remove from heat and stir in:
   - ¼ cup togarashi spice blend (see headnote)

3. ALLOW the oil to cool to room temperature, then refrigerate.

YIELD: 1½ CUPS

STORAGE: The oil will keep in the refrigerator for up to 7 days.

SEASONED RICE WINE VINEGAR

We use our seasoned rice wine vinegar to "wake up" dishes that need a little more pop. The well-balanced blend of salt, sweet, and acid also brings balance to many of our Asian dressings and sauces — so many that we don't have the space to name them all here!

1. COMBINE in a small saucepan over medium heat:
    - 1 cup rice wine vinegar
    - 2 tablespoons salt
    - 4 tablespoons sugar or mild honey

2. STIR gently until salt and sugar are dissolved. Remove pan from heat and stir in:
    - 1 tablespoon sake (optional)

3. COOL completely, then store, covered, in refrigerator.

YIELD: 1¼ CUPS

STORAGE: Vinegar will keep in the refrigerator for up to 1 year.

SZECHUAN OIL

This oil has a deep, rich taste and color, and we use its nutty, earthy spice to emphasize the unique flavor of Szechuan cuisine. It works well in **Chinese Chicken Salad** (page 36), **Dan Dan Noodles** (page 50), and **Coriander Shrimp Chow Fun** (page 92).

1. COMBINE in a small saucepan over medium heat:
   - 1 cup neutral cooking oil
   - ½ cup gochugaru (page 164)
   - 3 tablespoons toasted sesame seeds
   - 4 star anise pods
   - 2 bay leaves
   - 2 teaspoons ground coriander
   - 1½ teaspoons ground cumin
   - ¼ teaspoon curry powder
   - 4 cloves garlic, grated

2. BRING ingredients just to a boil, and then reduce heat and simmer for 3 to 4 minutes (don't let the spices burn). Remove from heat and stir in:
   - 2 tablespoons whole Szechuan peppercorns, tied in a sachet

3. WAIT 10 seconds, then stir in:
   - 2 tablespoons soy sauce

YIELD: 1½ CUPS

STORAGE: The oil will keep for at least 14 days.

EVERYDAY
EQUIPMENT

CARBON-STEEL PAN. For reasons that escape us, the carbon-steel pan has yet to catch on in American home kitchens, but many restaurant kitchens prize them for their utility and sturdiness. Once a new pan has been well seasoned with oil, the carbon steel is naturally nonstick (no synthetic coating), and it holds heat and sears better than stainless steel at half the price!

FISH SPATULA. A fish spatula has a flexible thin metal body with a slightly sharp edge that slides easily under fish that is cooking in a pan. It dramatically reduces damage to the fish caused by bits sticking to the pan.

JAPANESE MANDOLINE. The Benriner Japanese mandoline is a time-saving marvel of good design and economy. Most serious professional cooks keep one in their knife kit, as it really is the best way to evenly slice or julienne many types of vegetables. In essence, the mandoline contains a sharp, lightweight blade fixed to a plastic body, and the height of the cutting surface can be adjusted. You can quickly make dozens of perfectly even slices by sliding a vegetable back and forth across the blade. Through personal experience, we highly recommend using the finger guard.

KNIVES. While knives come in a million shapes and sizes, the vast majority of knifework in this book can be accomplished with a chef's knife and a paring knife. Which brand of knife is a matter of personal preference. Most of us at Coco prefer Japanese knives over German ones. Japanese knives tend to be more nimble and lightweight, while German knives tend to be heavier, sturdier, and much more tolerant of abuse.

MICROPLANE GRATER. Microplane is the trademarked name of the most popular line of very fine food graters/zesters. They are perfect for grating fluffy, delicate cheese over pastas, and they work just as well for zesting citrus without removing the bitter pith at the same time.

MULTIUSE ELECTRIC COOKER (INSTANT POT). Multicookers like the Instant Pot are relatively new in the cooking world, but they are finding growing popularity across the globe for an impressive number of possible applications — from pressure cooker to slow cooker, rice cooker, sauté pan, and food warmer. It is worth noting that the Instant Pot is a useful kitchen tool that can save time and space, but nothing can replace the time-tested traditional methods of cooking, where you can see, hear, smell, and taste things as you cook them. What the Instant Pot does incredibly well is deliver clean, reliable heat that can shave hours off time-intensive cooking projects. The practical result is that dinners that would otherwise be out of reach of many families suddenly become attainable. Braising ribs takes less than 1 hour (instead of 4), and ramen broth that would otherwise take all day can now be made in 2 hours!

RICE COOKER. The automatic rice cooker is, without hyperbole, one of the most important additions to cooking in the last 80 years. Well over a billion people use rice cookers each day because of their "set it and forget it" utility; untold tons of rice have been saved from scorching by the automatic shutoff feature. The rice cooker saves valuable stovetop space and keeps the rice warm for hours after it is done cooking.

EVERYDAY
INGREDIENTS

Where to Buy

An important, and often over-looked, factor in creating powerful, vibrant flavors is the freshness of your spices. The difference between a fresh spice and one that has sat in a plastic jar at the supermarket for years is, without hyperbole, like night and day. When you find a supplier that can reliably provide you with spices that contain life and strength, keep going back to them!

We trust Oaktown Spice Shop in Oakland, California, without hesitation, and they have a robust and reliable online store. They know their trade inside and out, and they supply some of the country's greatest restaurants.

It is worth noting, however, that if you have independent specialty shops or international foods markets in your area, there really is no substitute for speaking face to face with someone who has first-hand expertise in the ingredients you want to use. These independent shop owners can answer questions on seasonality and availability, and they can order products to better suit your needs in a way that the large-scale Internet retailers just can't.

Spices

GOCHUGARU. A cornerstone of Korean cuisine, gochugaru is made by drying red chilis in the sun. Without it, kimchi wouldn't taste like kimchi, and we would not have gochujang! It is moderately spicy and has a sweet, smoky aspect as well.

STAR ANISE. Native to China but used throughout Asia, star anise has a licorice-like flavor. The star-shaped pods are added whole during the cooking process and then removed before serving.

SZECHUAN PEPPERCORNS. Also known as prickly ash, Szechuan peppercorns are a commonly used spice in certain Chinese cuisines. They have a truly distinct flavor, and if you've ever had spicy Chinese food that leaves you with a tingling, numbing feeling in your mouth, you've experienced Szechuan peppercorns.

TOGARASHI. This is a Japanese spice blend that contains red chile pepper, roasted orange peel, ground ginger, white and black sesame seeds, poppy seeds, nori, and Szechuan pepper. It has a slightly nutty, slightly spicy profile in oils and infusions. We use it to make a tasty crust on fish, or we even just sprinkle it on a bowl of rice.

VADOUVAN CURRY POWDER. This is a French take on curry powder. In addition to the normal cast of characters that you find in curry powder — like ginger, garlic, cardamom, and nutmeg — vadouvan curry contains dried shallots. It has a slightly sweeter, elegant, and almost whimsical profile as compared to other curry powders.

WHITE PEPPER. White pepper comes from the same plant as black pepper. The berries are just allowed to ripen further, and the outer husk is removed to reveal white peppercorns. White pepper is widely used in Asian, Indian, and Mexican cuisines and has an earthier taste.

Sauces and Pastes

CHINESE SESAME PASTE. People often try to substitute tahini for Chinese sesame paste, but they have very different flavors. The Chinese version features sesame seeds that have been roasted longer for a darker, thicker product. Often, the paste and oil will have separated in the jar and will need to be mixed up before use.

DOUBAN CHILI PASTE. Also known as broad bean paste, or toban-djan, douban bean paste is a distinctive flavor of Szechuan cooking. It brings a unique character and spiciness to noodle dishes and stir-fried tofu.

FISH SAUCE. Fish sauce is a powerful and pungent condiment that is pivotal to making authentic Southeast Asian food. Put simply, it is the liquid reserved from the process of salting and fermenting fish, most commonly anchovies. A little goes a long way in salad dressings and dipping sauces to impart an unmistakable salty flavor. We recommend Red Boat brand.

GOCHUJANG. Another important ingredient that features prominently in Korean cooking, gochujang is a spicy fermented soy bean and red pepper paste. Gochujang can be too intense for most people to use straight, so it is generally mixed with rice wine vinegar, soy sauce, and sesame before it hits the plate. There really isn't a substitute for its breathy, funky profile in Korean cooking.

HOISIN. This Chinese sauce is made from soybeans, sugar, and spices like star anise, garlic, and chili powder. It is dark and thick, and it is typically paired with meats and seafood. Sometimes referred to as Peking sauce, you'll always see it with crispy Peking duck!

KECAP MANIS. This Indonesian sweet soy sauce is great for marinades and glazes. Imagine using it like you would maple syrup or honey for sweetness that also adds salt.

OYSTER SAUCE. Along with hoisin and plum sauce, oyster sauce contributes a great deal to Chinese cooking. While it can be difficult to find the ingredients list on some of these products, take time to find an oyster sauce that contains only oysters as opposed to chicken and extra sugar. The search for a proper one will pay off with a lighter and more distinctive punch of umami.

PLUM SAUCE. This truly classic sweet and sour condiment from China is made with plums or other fruit, sugar, vinegar, ginger, and chiles.

RED MISO. Red miso is produced with a higher proportion of fermented soybeans than white miso and is aged much longer. It is more pungent and salty, and it is best suited for deep, rich soups and sauces.

SAMBAL OELEK. You can purchase this spicy Southeast Asian chili sauce at any Asian market. The consistency is thicker than that of a puréed hot sauce. It also contains minimal acid or vinegar, so you can use it to add heat without affecting other aspects of your food.

TAMARI. Both tamari and soy sauce are derived from fermented soybeans and have similar flavors, but tamari contains little or no wheat, depending on the brand. Tamari can be used to add that salty, umami taste that you get from soy sauce while avoiding gluten.

TAMARIND PASTE. This strong, condensed paste is made from the sticky sour fruit of the tamarind tree. It is usually combined with a sweetener to create a unique sweet and sour flavor found in Southeast Asian food from Thailand and Vietnam. The paste is soaked in water to make tamarind juice.

THAI CURRY PASTE. Thai curry pastes are generally made with fresh chiles, lemongrass, galangal or ginger, garlic, shallot, lime leaves, and shrimp paste. The color of the chiles determines the appearance and spice level of the curry paste. Green pastes tend to be spicier than red or yellow ones. We generally pick Thai curry pastes that don't include shrimp to avoid any dietary restrictions or allergies.

THAI SWEET CHILI SAUCE. This is made by cooking down garlic, chiles, sugar, and salt. There are a number of great bottled products available, and we have used it as a secret weapon for brightening up sauces for years.

WHITE MISO. We like white miso, or shiro, for dressings and marinades because it has a nutty and delicate profile. It is definitely on the milder side. Traditionally, miso is produced by fermenting soybeans and rice or barley. More recently we've seen miso made with chickpeas, so people with soy sensitivities do have options.

Vinegars and Oil

MIRIN. Japanese cooking would be vastly different without this sweet rice wine. It has more sugar and less alcohol than sake and makes all sorts of iconic Japanese dishes possible, from teriyaki sauce to ramen.

SEASONED RICE WINE VINEGAR. This rice vinegar has added sugar and salt to produce a well-balanced tangy, salty, sweet flavor. It is great for salad dressings and Asian sauces. You can purchase it or make your own (see recipe on page 157).

SESAME OIL. Light sesame oil is suitable to use for frying, as it has a high smoke point. The recipes in this book call for a darker, toasted sesame oil that imparts a rich nutty aspect to dishes.

Dried Produce and Seafood

BONITO FLAKES. This is an essential ingredient in dashi, a Japanese soup stock. It is made by fermenting and drying, then smoking bonito fish.

DRIED SCALLOPS. These have a highly concentrated and intense flavor of the sea. Dried scallops add a salty, umami-rich depth to Japanese and Chinese cuisines.

DRIED SHIITAKE MUSHROOMS. An essential part of Asian cooking, dried shiitakes have a deep, savory flavor that contribute body and depth to vegetarian dishes.

KIZAME NORI. Shredded form of nori used in Japanese dishes.

KOMBU. This is a type of dried kelp found primarily in Japanese cooking. Most commonly it is used to make dashi, or soup stock.

NORI. This Japanese word describes sheets of dried edible seaweed used to wrap rice in sushi rolls and also to flavor soups and noodle dishes. Toasted and seasoned nori sheets have become a popular snack in the United States, and they can be found in most supermarkets.

Fresh Produce and Dairy

BEAN SPROUTS. Mung bean sprouts are a sprouted vegetable used widely in Asian cultures. They have a light, crispy texture and they take on the flavors of other ingredients quite readily. They are often stir-fried, but they work well raw in salads or blanched and seasoned.

CRÈME FRAÎCHE. This rich, thick cultured cream has a tart, nutty flavor. It can be used as a base for creamy salad dressings, whipped for desserts, or added to soups for more body and depth.

DAIKON RADISH. Daikon is a white radish with a crisp and mild flavor. It works great in salads and can be pickled or stir-fried to add a refreshing crunch to Asian dishes.

KABOCHA SQUASH. Often described as tasting like a cross between a pumpkin and a sweet potato, kabocha is a Japanese squash with a light, fluffy texture when cooked. It is often cut into thin wedges and tempura fried, roasted, or steamed to bring out its sweetness.

MEYER LEMONS. Smaller and more delicate than regular lemons, Meyer lemons have a much sweeter and more complex flavor. They are thought to be a cross between a lemon and a mandarin orange, and even if that is not true, it is a great way to describe them!

RICOTTA SALATA. This is produced by salting and pressing fresh ricotta to remove water and create a firmer texture and more concentrated flavor. More often than not, ricotta salata is used as a "finishing cheese" cheese, grated or shaved over the top of dishes as an accent or even as a striking garnish.

Noodles

FLAT RICE NOODLES. Flat rice noodles come in various widths. Phad Thai works best with medium-width noodles, and chow fun works best with the wide ones. Dried rice noodles cook very quickly, so be sure to read the directions carefully.

HO FUN NOODLES. Ho fun or shahe fen are a type of wide rice noodles from southern China. Typically used in a dish called chow fun, they are sold fresh in large sheets that are sliced into strips before cooking. They must be used within a couple of days for best results.

LO MEIN NOODLES. These egg noodles are often referred to as lo mein noodles, after the Chinese dish they are most associated with. Dried versions are available, though it is worth the extra effort to source fresh egg noodles. They freeze well for up to 3 months, so buy extra when you find them.

RAMEN NOODLES. Ramen noodles are made with flour, water, salt, and an alkaline bicarbonate that gives them a unique springiness and mouthfeel. We love fresh ramen noodles, but in a pinch there are lots of quality dried options on the market.

Other Ingredients

COCONUT MILK. Coconut milk is primarily sold in cans in the United States. It is thick, slightly sweet, and very creamy. It factors heavily in Southeast Asian and Caribbean cuisine.

COCONUT NECTAR. Coconut nectar is the sweet sap from the sugar blossoms that grow in the canopies of coconut groves. It does not have a strong coconut flavor, unlike coconut milk and other coconut products.

MASA HARINA. This Mexican flour is made from dried corn and used to make tortillas, tamales, and other masa-based dishes.

PALM SUGAR. Palm sugar is the sweetener of choice in Southeast Asia. It is processed from the crystalized sap of palm trees. It has a deep, nutty sweetness and is essential for producing Southeast Asian dishes that are truly authentic.

SILKEN TOFU. Also called silk tofu or Japanese tofu, silken tofu has a much more delicate texture and consistency than regular tofu. It is generally packaged in aseptic boxes that don't need to be kept cold, so look for it outside the cooler on grocery store shelves. Silken tofu can be blended for a thick, creamy texture that can be used for salad dressings or even vegan dressings.

THANK YOU

WE ARE SO THANKFUL

for the people who helped make this book a reality — those who helped make us the cooks we are, and our friends and family who supported us along the way.

Thank you, Miranda Brown, for so diligently developing and testing recipes over the years. Thank you, Laura Briggs, for keeping the restaurant on the rails when we can't, and Donn Boulanger, for bringing grace and beauty everywhere you go. Thank you Deanna Cook, Carolyn Eckert, Sarah Guare, and everyone else at Storey, and of course, Ann Lewis and Joe Keller — this book simply doesn't exist without all of you.

Thank you to all the cooks who have informed how we move, think, and speak in a kitchen: Alice Waters, Kirk Weber, Josiah Citrin, Nancy Oaks, Julya Shin, Chris Lee, Rob Watson, Rico Rivera, and John Henson. We also thank Xander Pirdy, Aaron Thayer, and Joe Gionfriddo for raising the bar for us. To Jesus, Stephen, Eric, Al and Dave, Tanner and Adam, and everyone at Coco — thank you.

To our friends and family — Leon and Sunny, Jacobus and Ali, Moria and Ben, Barbara and Dave, Dad, Chuck, Oma, Abuji and Louise, Deborah and Nick, Ben and Cory, Frank and Christine, Nate and Amanda, Ken and Hortensia, Mikey and Colby, Dillon, Kyle and Libby, Dan and Charlie, Katie and Aletheia, Gabe, John and Patty, Donna, Ellen and Natan, Brownie, Sanford D'Amato, Christina Barber-Just, Joanne Weir, Virginia Willis, Lisa and Sally Ekus, Kitchen Garden Farm, Grandpa Nate, Grandma Faye, and Grandma Carmen — we love you all.

INDEX

Page numbers in *italic* indicate photos.

A

almonds
    Chinese Chicken Salad, 36, *37*
arugula
    Honey Miso Noodle Salad, 28, *29*
    Orange, Mango, and Avocado Salad, 32, *33*
Asian pear
    Grilled Shrimp, Asian Pear, and Watercress Salad, 24, *24*, *25*
Avocado Salad, Orange, Mango, and, 32, *33*

B

balance. *See* flavor balance
basil
    Salmon and Green Thai Curry Rice Bowl, 108, *109*
beans, canned
    Chili Con Carne, 104, *105*
bean sprouts, 167
    Bibimbap, 78, *78*, *79*
    East-West Rice Bowl, 72, *73*
    Salmon Teriyaki Bento Box, 116, *117*
    Seasoned Bean Sprouts, 140, *141*
    Shiitake Mushroom and Tofu Phad Thai, 119–121, *119*, *121*
beef
    Bibimbap, 78, *78*, *79*
    Chili Con Carne, 104, *105*
    Short-Rib Tacos, Grilled, 76, *77*
Bento Box, Salmon Teriyaki, 116, *117*
Bibimbap, 78, *78*, *79*
bok choy
    East-West Rice Bowl, 72, *73*
bonito flakes, 167
    Dashi, 62, *62*
    Shoyu Ramen Broth and Tare, 60–63, *61*, *62*, *63*
Broccoli Salad, 40, *41*

    General Tso's Tofu, 96, *97*
    Salmon Teriyaki Bento Box, 116, *117*
broth, *18. See also* Shoyu Ramen Broth
burritos, Thai, 107

C

cabbage
    Chinese Chicken Salad, 36, *37*
    Grilled Short Rib Tacos, 76, *77*
    Honey Miso Noodle Salad, 28, *29*
    Kimchi, Quick, *144*, 145
    Pork Carnitas Tacos, 54–55, *54*, *55*
    Thai Cabbage, 132, *133*
    Zesty Jalapeño Cabbage Slaw, 44, *44*, *45*
carrots
    Bibimbap, 78, *78*, *79*
    Honey Miso Noodle Salad, 28, *29*
    Salmon Teriyaki Bento Box, 116, *117*
    Seasoned Carrots, 140, *141*
cheese
    Macaroni and Cheese, 124, *125*
    Mornay, 122, *123*
chicken
    Chinese Chicken Salad, 36, *37*
    Clay Pot Miso Chicken, 58–59, *59*
    Coco Shoyu Ramen, *64*, 65
    East-West Rice Bowl, 72, *73*
    Honey Miso Noodle Salad, 28, *29*
    Shoyu Ramen Broth and Tare, 60–63, *61*, *62*, *63*
    skewers, 115
    Thai Chicken Rice Bowl, 82, *82*, *83*
Chile Oil, 154, *155*
Chili Con Carne, 104, *105*
Chinese Chicken Salad, 36, *37*
Chive Oil, 154, *155*
Chow Fun Sauce, 90, 91
    Coriander Shrimp Chow Fun, 92, *93*

cilantro
    Grilled Short Rib Tacos, 76, *77*
    Salsa Verde, Cilantro, *102*, 103
    Shiitake Mushroom and Tofu Phad Thai, 119–121, *119, 121*
Coco (restaurant), 13–19, *13*
Coco Shoyu Ramen, *64*, 65
coconut milk, 169
    Green Thai Curry, *106*, 107
    Peanut Sauce, Thai, *80*, 81
    Vegan Coconut Curry, *98*, 99
coconut nectar, 169
    Phad Thai Sauce, 118, *118*
cod
    Miso-Glazed Cod Rice Bowl, 112, *113*
Coriander Shrimp Chow Fun, 92, *93*
corn, 31
    Chili Con Carne, 104, *105*
crème fraîche, 167
    Lime Shallot Crème Fraîche, 130, *131*
Cucumber Pickles, Xander's, 146, *147*
    Bibimbap, 78, *78*, 79
    Chinese Chicken Salad, 36, *37*
    Salmon Teriyaki Bento Box, 116, *117*
curry
    Green Thai Curry, *106*, 107
    Salmon and Green Thai Curry Rice Bowl, 108, *109*
    Vegan Coconut Curry, *98*, 99

D

daikon radish, 167
    Shiitake Mushroom and Tofu Phad Thai, 119–121, *119, 121*
Dan Dan noodles, 50, *51*
Dashi, *18*, 60, *61, 62, 62*
dip, dressing as, 26, *26*
douban chili paste, 165
    Peanut Sauce, Spicy Szechuan, *48*, 49
    Spicy Miso Paste, 128, *129*
dressings, 21. See also vinaigrettes
    Honey Miso Dressing, 26, *26*, 27
    Jalapeño Lime Dressing, *30*, 31
    Korean Hot Pepper Dressing, *22*, 23
    Togarashi Dressing, *38, 39, 39*
dried products, 167, *167*

E

eggs/egg whites
    Bibimbap, 78, *78, 79*
    Coco Shoyu Ramen, *64*, 65
    General Tso's Tofu, 96, *97*
    Soy-Cured Eggs, 136, *136, 137*
equipment, everyday, 160–61, *160, 161*

F

fish. *See* cod; salmon
fish sauce, 165, *165*
    Phad Thai Sauce, 118, *118*
    Thai Curry, Green, *106*, 107
flavor balance, 14
    sauces and, 18, *19*

G

garlic
    Kimchi, Quick, *144*, 145
    Shoyu Ramen Broth and Tare, 60–63, *61, 62, 63*
    Spicy Miso Paste, 128, *129*
    Vegan Coconut Curry, *98*, 99
General Tso's Sauce, 94, 95
    General Tso's Tofu, 96, *97*
ginger
    General Tso's Sauce, 94, 95
    Ginger Oil, 152, *153*
    Orange Ginger Vinaigrette, *34, 35, 35*
    Pickled Ginger, 152, *153*
    Pickled Shiitake Mushrooms, *148*, 149
    Ponzu, *110*, 111
    Scallion Ginger Jam, 56, *56*, 57
    Shoyu Ramen Broth and Tare, 60–63, *61, 62, 63*
    Spicy Miso Paste, 128, *129*
gochugaru, 164
    Szechuan Oil, 158, *159*
gochujang, 165
    Hot Pepper Sauce, Korean, 74, *75*
    Korean Hot Pepper Sauce, 74, *75*

H

hoisin sauce, 165
    Hoisin Barbecue Sauce, 66, *67*
    Hoisin-Glazed Baby Back Ribs, 68, *68, 69*
    Plum Sauce, *70*, 71
honey
    Barbecue Sauce, Hoisin, 66, *67*
    Honey Miso Dressing, 26, *26, 27*
    Honey Miso Noodle Salad, 28, *29*
    Hot Pepper Sauce, Korean, 74, *75*
    Seasoned Rice Wine Vinegar, 157, *157*

I

ingredients, everyday, 162–69
    dried products and seafood, 167
    fresh produce and dairy, 167–68
    noodles, 168
    other, 169
    sauces and pastes, 164–66, *165*
    spices, 164
    vinegars and oil, 166
Instant Pot, 161, *161*

J

jalapeños
    Jalapeño Lime Dressing, *30*, 31
    Ponzu, *110*, 111
    Zesty Jalapeño Cabbage Slaw, 44, *44, 45*
Jam, Scallion Ginger, 56, *56, 57*
Japanese Turnips, Pickled, 150, *151*
joy, cooking and, 15

K

kabocha squash, 167
    Kabocha Squash and Tofu Rice Bowl, Steamed, 100, *101*
kaffir lime leaves
    Green Thai Curry, *106*, 107
    Vegan Coconut Curry, *98*, 99
Kalbi Marinade, 134, *134, 135*
    Short-Rib Tacos, Grilled, 76, *77*

kale, curly green
    Clay Pot Miso Chicken, 58–59, *59*
kecap manis, 165
    General Tso's Sauce, *94*, 95
kelp. *See* Dashi
ketchup, 16
    Barbecue Sauce, Hoisin, 66, *67*
kimchi
    Bibimbap, 78, *78*, *79*
    Kimchi, Quick, *144*, 145
kiwi
    Kalbi Marinade, 134, *134*, *135*
kombu (dried kelp), 167
    Shoyu Ramen Broth and Tare, *60*,
      60–63, *61*, *63*
Korean Bolognese, 84, 85
    Korean Sloppy Joes, 88, *89*
Korean Hot Pepper Dressing, *22*, 23
Korean Hot Pepper Sauce, 74, *75*
    Korean Bolognese, *84*, 85
Korean Sloppy Joes, 88, *89*
Korean Spaghetti, 86, *87*

L

lemons/lemon juice
    Meyer lemons, 150, 168
    Pickled Japanese Turnips, 150, *151*
lettuce
    Thai Chicken Rice Bowl, 82, *82*, *83*
    for wraps, 78
limes/lime juice. *See also* kaffir lime leaves
    Grilled Short Rib Tacos, 76, *77*
    Jalapeño Lime Dressing, *30*, 31
    Korean Hot Pepper Dressing, *22*, 23
    Lime Shallot Crème Fraîche, 130, *131*
    Ponzu, *110*, 111
    Shiitake Mushroom and Tofu Phad Thai,
      119–121, *119*, *121*
    Thai Curry, Green, *106*, 107

M

Macaroni and Cheese, 124, *125*
mangos
    Orange, Mango, and Avocado Salad,
      32, *33*

marinade
    Kalbi Marinade, 134, *134*, *135*
    Miso Marinade, *138*, 139
masa harina, 169
    Chili Con Carne, 104, *105*
mirin, *165*, 166
    Clay Pot Miso Chicken, 58–59, *59*
    Miso Marinade, *138*, 139
    Ponzu, *110*, 111
    Teriyaki Sauce, *114*, 115
miso, 165, 166
    Clay Pot Miso Chicken, 58–59, *59*
    Honey Miso Dressing, 26, *26*, *27*
    Honey Miso Noodle Salad, 28, *29*
    Miso-Glazed Cod Rice Bowl, 112, *113*
    Miso Marinade, *138*, 139
    Spicy Miso Paste, 128, *129*
Mornay, 122, *123*
    Macaroni and Cheese, 124, *124*, *125*
mushrooms. *See* shiitake mushrooms
mustard greens
    Clay Pot Miso Chicken, 58–59, *59*

N

noodles, 168, *169*. *See also* pasta; ramen
    Coriander Shrimp Chow Fun, 92, *93*
    Dan Dan noodles, 50, *51*
    Honey Miso Noodle Salad, 28, *29*
    Shiitake Mushroom and Tofu Phad Thai,
      119–121, *119*, *121*
nori, 167, *167*
    Coco Shoyu Ramen, *64*, 65

O

oils, 127, 153, 166
    Chile Oil, 154, *155*
    Chive Oil, 154, *155*
    Ginger Oil, 152, *153*
    Szechuan Oil, 158, *159*
    vinegars and, 166
onions. *See also* scallions; shallots
    Pickled White Onions, 142, *143*
    Thai Chicken Rice Bowl, 82, *82*, *83*
    Zesty Jalapeño Cabbage Slaw, 44, *44*,
      45

oranges/orange juice/orange zest
    Hoisin Barbecue Sauce, 66, *67*
    Orange, Mango, and Avocado Salad,
      32, *33*
    Orange Ginger Vinaigrette, *34*, 35, *35*
oyster sauce, 165, *165*
    Chow Fun Sauce, 90, *91*
    Plum Sauce, *70*, 71

P

palm sugar, 169
    Thai Curry, Green, *106*, 107
    Vegan Coconut Curry, *98*, 99
panko
    General Tso's Tofu, 96, *97*
    Macaroni and Cheese, 124, *125*
pasta
    Macaroni and Cheese, 124, *125*
    Spaghetti, Korean, 86, *87*
peanut butter
    Peanut Sauce, Spicy Szechuan, *48*, 49
    Peanut Sauce, Thai, *80*, 81
peanuts
    Shiitake Mushroom and Tofu Phad Thai,
      119–121, *119*, *121*
pea shoots
    Coriander Shrimp Chow Fun, 92, *93*
Phad Thai, Shiitake Mushroom and Tofu,
    119–121, *119*, *121*
Phad Thai Sauce, 118, *118*
    Shiitake Mushroom and Tofu Phad Thai,
      119–121, *119*, *121*
Pickled Ginger, 152, *153*
Pickled Japanese Turnips, 150, *151*
Pickled Shiitake Mushrooms, *148*, 149
Pickled White Onions, 142, *143*
Pickles, Xander's Cucumber, 146, *147*
pineapple
    Salsa, Manchamanteles, 52, 53
pine nuts
    Broccoli Salad, 40, *41*
planning, cooking and, 15
plate construction. *See* presentation of food
plum sauce, 165
    East-West Rice Bowl, 72, *73*
    Plum Sauce, 70, 71, *71*

Ponzu, *110*, 111
    Cod Rice Bowl, Miso-Glazed, 112, *113*
pork
    Baby Back Ribs, Hoisin-Glazed, 68, *68*, *69*
    Korean Bolognese, *84*, 85
    Peanut Sauce, Spicy Szechuan, *48*, 49
    Shoyu Ramen Broth and Tare, 60–63, *61*, *62*, *63*
    Tacos, Carnitas Pork, 54–55, *54*, *55*
potatoes
    Lime Shallot Crème Fraîche, 130, *131*
presentation of food, 15, 24, *24*, *25*
produce, fresh, 167–68. *See also specific product*

R

ramen, 18, 168
    Coco Shoyu Ramen, *64*, 65
    dry noodles, using, 65
    Shoyu Ramen Broth and Tare, 60–63, *60*, *61*, *62*, *63*
Red Wine Vinaigrette, *42*, 43
rice
    Bibimbap, 78, *78*, *79*
    Chicken Rice Bowl, Thai, 82, *82*, *83*
    Clay Pot Miso Chicken, 58–59, *59*
    Cod Rice Bowl, Miso-Glazed, 112, *113*
    East-West Rice Bowl, 72, *73*
    General Tso's Tofu, 96, *97*
    Hoisin-Glazed Baby Back Ribs, 68, *69*
    Kabocha Squash and Tofu Rice Bowl, Steamed, 100, *101*
    Salmon and Green Thai Curry Rice Bowl, 108, *109*
    Salmon Teriyaki Bento Box, 116, *117*
    topping for, *22*, 23
rice cooker, 161, *161*
rice wine vinegar. *See* Seasoned Rice Wine Vinegar
ricotta salata, 32, 168

S

sake
    Miso Marinade, *138*, 139
    Shoyu Tare, 63, *63*
    Teriyaki Sauce, *114*, 115
salads, 21
    Broccoli Salad, 40, *41*
    Chinese Chicken Salad, 36, *37*
    Grilled Shrimp, Asian Pear, and Watercress Salad, 24, *24*, *25*
    Honey Miso Noodle Salad, 28, *29*
    Orange, Mango, and Avocado Salad, 32, *33*
    Zesty Jalapeño Cabbage Slaw, 44, *44*, *45*
salmon
    Salmon and Green Thai Curry Rice Bowl, 108, *109*
    Salmon Teriyaki Bento Box, 116, *117*
salsa
    Salsa, Manchamanteles, *52*, 53
    Salsa Verde, Cilantro, *102*, 103
sambal oelek, 165, *165*
    Hoisin Barbecue Sauce, 66, *67*
sauces, 47. *See also* salsa
    Barbecue Sauce, Hoisin, 66, *67*
    Chow Fun Sauce, *90*, 91
    flavor balance and, 18, *19*
    General Tso's Sauce, *94*, 95
    Hot Pepper Sauce, Korean, 74, *75*
    Korean Bolognese, *84*, 85
    Mornay, 122, *123*
    pastes and, 164–66, *165*
    Peanut Sauce, Spicy Szechuan, *48*, 49
    Peanut Sauce, Thai, *80*, 81
    Phad Thai Sauce, 118, *118*
    Plum Sauce, 70, 71, *71*
    Ponzu, *110*, 111
    Salsa, Manchamanteles, 52, 53
    Scallion Ginger Jam, 56, *56*, *57*
    Teriyaki Sauce, *114*, 115
scallions
    Chinese Chicken Salad, 36, *37*
    East-West Rice Bowl, 72, *73*
    Scallion Ginger Jam, 56, *56*, *57*
    Shoyu Ramen Broth and Tare, 60–63, *61*, *62*, *63*

scallops, dried, 167
    Dashi, 62, *62*
    Shoyu Ramen Broth and Tare, 60–63, *61*, *62*, *63*
seafood, 167. *See also* scallops, dried; shrimp
seasoned rice wine vinegar, 12, *12*, 166
Seasoned Rice Wine Vinegar, 157, *157*
seasoning, 13–14
secret ingredient. *See* seasoned rice wine vinegar
sesame seeds
    Chinese Chicken Salad, 36, *37*
    East-West Rice Bowl, 72, *73*
    Hoisin Barbecue Sauce, 66, *67*
    Hoisin-Glazed Baby Back Ribs, 68, *69*
    Honey Miso Noodle Salad, 28, *29*
    Kalbi Marinade, 134, *134*, *135*
    Kimchi, Quick, *144*, 145
    Korean Hot Pepper Dressing, *22*, 23
    Szechuan Oil, 158, *159*
    Togarashi Oil, 156, *156*
shallots
    Lime Shallot Crème Fraîche, 130, *131*
shiitake mushrooms
    Clay Pot Miso Chicken, 58–59, *59*
    dried, *166*, 167
    Pickled Shiitake Mushrooms, *148*, 149
    Shiitake Mushroom and Tofu Phad Thai, 119–121, *119*, *121*
Shoyu Ramen Broth, 60–62, *60*, *61*
Shoyu Tare, *61*, 63, *63*
    Coco Shoyu Ramen, *64*, 65
shrimp
    Coriander Shrimp Chow Fun, 92, *93*
    Grilled Shrimp, Asian Pear, and Watercress Salad, 24, *24*, *25*
Sloppy Joes, Korean, 88, *89*
soup, 100, *100*
soy sauce, 165
    Chow Fun Sauce, *90*, 91
    General Tso's Sauce, *94*, 95
    Kalbi Marinade, 134, *134*, *135*
    Shoyu Ramen Broth and Tare, 60–63, *61*, *62*, *63*
    Soy-Cured Eggs, 136, *136*, *137*
    Teriyaki Sauce, *114*, 115

Spaghetti, Korean, 86, *87*
spices, 164
squash. *See* kabocha squash
star anise, 164
    Szechuan Oil, 158, *159*
    Vegan Coconut Curry, *98*, 99
stir-fries, 66
sushi rolls, 39
sweeteners, alternative, 14, *14*
Szechuan Oil, 158, *159*
Szechuan Peanut Sauce, Spicy, *48*, 49
Szechuan pepper, 164
    Szechuan Oil, 158, *159*

T

tacos
    Carnitas Pork Tacos, 54–55, *54*, *55*
    Grilled Short Rib Tacos, 76, *77*
    taco night, 104
tamari, 166
    Ponzu, *110*, 111
tamarind juice
    homemade, 118
    Phad Thai Sauce, 118, *118*
tamarind paste, 166
    Tamarind Juice, Homemade, 118
tare, *18*, 60, *61*, 63, *63*, 65 . *See also* Shoyu Tare
teriyaki
    Salmon Teriyaki Bento Box, 116, *117*
    Teriyaki Sauce, *114*, 115
Thai Cabbage, 132, *133*
    Thai Chicken Rice Bowl, 82, *82*, *83*
Thai Chicken Rice Bowl, 82, *82*, *83*
Thai Curry, Green, *106*, 107
    Salmon and Green Thai Curry Rice
        Bowl, 108, *109*
Thai curry paste, 166
    Thai Curry, Green, *106*, 107
Thai Peanut Sauce, 80, 81
    Thai Chicken Rice Bowl, 82, *82*, *83*
Thai sweet chili sauce, 166
    Thai Cabbage, *132*, 133

tofu
    General Tso's Tofu, 96, *97*
    Kabocha Squash and Tofu Rice Bowl,
        Steamed, 100, *101*
    Shiitake Mushroom and Tofu Phad Thai,
        119–121, *119*, *121*
    silken, 169, *169*
Togarashi Oil, 156, *156*
    Togarashi Dressing, *38*, 39, *39*
tomatoes
    Chili Con Carne, 104, *105*
    Salsa, Manchamanteles, *52*, 53
    Vegan Coconut Curry, *98*, 99
tortillas, 72
    Grilled Short Rib Tacos, 76, *77*
    Pork Carnitas Tacos, 54–55, *54*, *55*
Turnips, Pickled Japanese, 150, *151*
    Cod Rice Bowl, Miso-Glazed, 112, *113*

U

umami, 16

V

Vegan Coconut Curry, *98*, 99
    Kabocha Squash and Tofu Rice Bowl,
        Steamed, 100, *101*
vinaigrettes
    Orange Ginger Vinaigrette, *34*, 35, *35*
    Red Wine Vinaigrette, *42*, 43
vinegars, 166

W

watercress
    Grilled Shrimp, Asian Pear, and
        Watercress Salad, 24, *24*, *25*